God's [love] in all things!

Love,
Smisers
& Wegdahls

10, 1983

The **ABC**'s
of Christian Mothering

The ABC's of
JAYNE

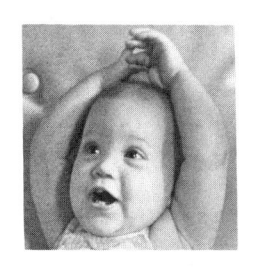

*A guide for
your baby's
first year*

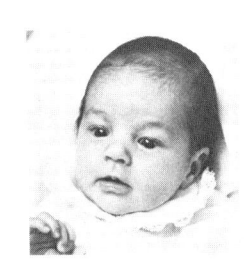

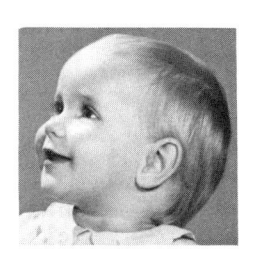

Christian Mothering

GARRISON

Tyndale House
Publishers, Inc.
Wheaton, Illinois

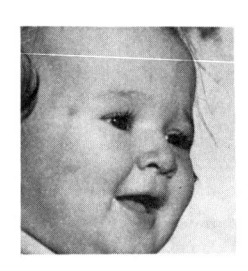

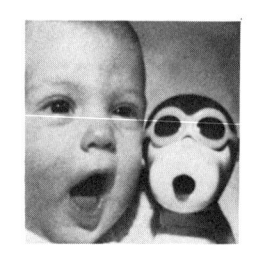

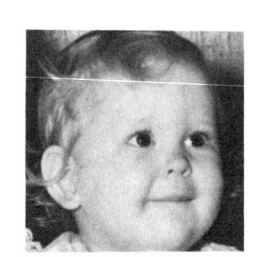

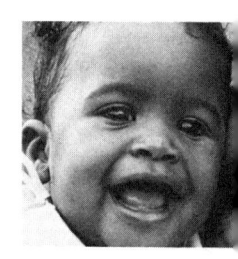

ACKNOWLEDGMENTS

Chess, Stella, "Are You Jealous of Your Children Without Knowing It?", *Family Circle*, November 1976.
Christenson, Larry, *The Christian Family*, Bethany Fellowship Inc., Minneapolis, 1970.
Crossley Hastings, *The Golden Sayings of Epictetus*, P. F. Collier and Son, New York, 1937.
Dodson, Fitzhugh, *How To Father*, Nash Publishing, Los Angeles, 1974.
Gibran, Kahlil, *The Prophet*, Alfred A. Knopf, New York, 1945.
Joseph, Michael, *Man Is the Only Animal That Blushes... Or Needs To*, Random House Inc., New York, 1970.
Spock, Benjamin, *Baby and Child Care*, Simon and Schuster Inc., New York, 1974.
Stevenson, Burton, *The Handbook of Shakespeare Quotations*, Charles Scribner's Sons, New York, 1937.
The Living Bible, Tyndale House Publishers, Wheaton, Illinois, 1971.

Grateful acknowledgment is given to *Scope* magazine (Vol. 17, January 1977, pp. 24, 25) for permission to quote chapter "Boredom: RX for the Housewife Blues." "Grandma: That Other Woman in Baby's Life" was first published in *Today's Christian Parent* (Vol. 19, Spring 1978, pp. 5, 6) and is reprinted here by permission.

In addition, I thank my husband, Olie, and my daughter, Heather, for their kindness and encouragement during the writing of this book.

Scripture quotations are from the King James Version, except for those marked TLB, which are from *The Living Bible*.

Library of Congress Catalog Card Number 79-66810. ISBN 0-8423-0016-3, cloth. Copyright © 1979 by Jayne Garrison. All rights reserved. First printing, November 1979. Printed in the United States of America.

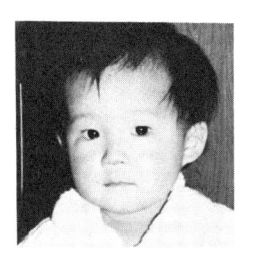

To Barbara E.

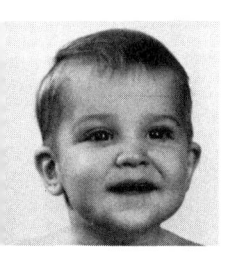

A
Adjustment—attitudes 11

Appearance—a more glorious you 12

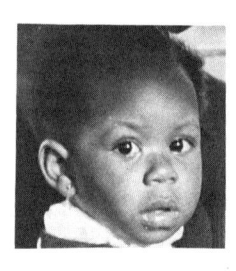

B
Baby-sitters—how to have a baby-sitter and your peace of mind too 17

Boredom—RX for the housewife blues 19

C
Church—the hallelujah hassle 23

Colic—temperamental tears 25

D
Dads—when proud papa becomes a passive father 29

Discipline—setting the stage for discipline 31

E
Emergencies—household SOS 35

Everyday things—bathing, diapering, and bedding your baby 37

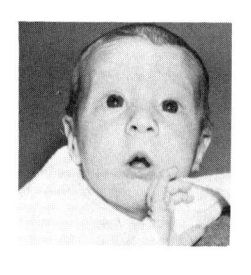

F
Feeding—food facts 43

Friends—Help! I'm lonely 46

G
Games—entertaining infants 49

Grandmothers—grandma: that other woman in baby's life 51

H
Helps—mother to mother 53

Housekeeping—checklist for a more livable house 55

I
Illness—temperature's rising 59

Ingenuity—the gift of love 62

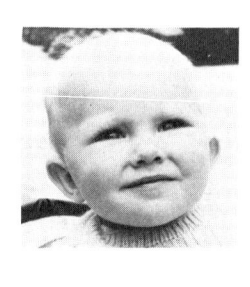

J
Jealousy—building on 65

Joy—joys of a woman 68

K
Keepsakes—making your own memory book 71

Kindness—the art of loving 73

L
Language—words of wisdom 75

Layette—size 0 77

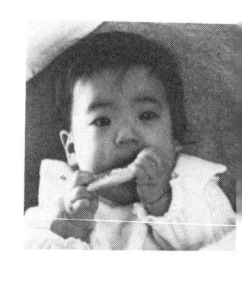

M
Meal planning—minute menus 83

Mistakes—when mom goofs up 85

N
Natural childbirth—all things considered 89

Nursing—a new look at an old art 94

O
Outings—going out with baby 97

Overweight—easy does it 98

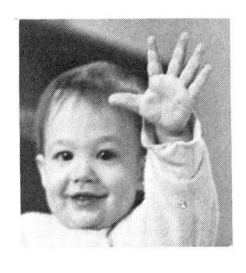

P
Pacifiers—the problem of "pacy" 101

Prayer—in praise of prayer 103

Q
Quality of mothering—time: quality or quantity? 105

Quiet time—Hi, God 107

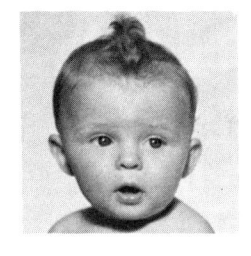

R
Reading—to the bookworm with love 109

Romance—when three's a crowd 110

S
Schedules—time out 113

Singing—homemaker's hymns 116

T
Toys—toy talk 119

Traveling—from here to there 120

U
Unhappiness—today is a happy day 123

Unity of family—playing fair 125

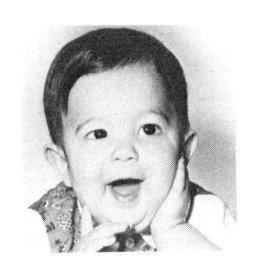

V
Vaccinations—keeping up with baby's health 129

Virtues—mom's a doll, or at least she ought to be 130

W
Weaning—a mother's bill of rights 133

Working—working out working 135

X, Y, Z
X, Y, Z's of family fun 139

This is a book about mothering
written by a mother.
All information and suggestions
are presented from the point of view
of personal experience and opinion.
Advice about medical and dietary matters
should be checked out
with your personal physician
or your baby's pediatrician.

Adjustment-attitudes

And the angel came in unto her, and said, Hail, thou that art highly favoured, the Lord is with thee: blessed art thou among women (Luke 1:28).

Congratulations—you are a mother, the most important person in the world to that tiny bundle of perfection. Right now, you are closer to God the Creator than any other creature, for you have joined with him to give birth to a new soul. And in the days ahead, your responsibilities will lie in the nurturing and training of this soul in the ways of the Lord. If you've had a chance to catch your breath and think about it, the whole idea can be pretty frightening.

Society will expect much from you as a mother. All successes and failures that your child should come by from this point on will be credited to "Dear Mom." But if the world expects much—you expect more.

I once attended a parenting seminar in which we were asked to describe a mother. The result was nothing short of ridiculous. "A mother," we said, "should be kind, intelligent, understanding, and supportive. She should create an atmosphere of mutual love and respect —always recognizing her duty to her child, but never forgetting herself or her husband." And then, as an afterthought, we added, "A mother should be perfect."

It may be too soon for you to have formed an opinion as to what a mother should be. Sometime during the year, however, you'll discover not only what a mother should be, but what she really is—a human being with limitations common to all mankind. God doesn't expect us to be superhuman. The very fact that he entrusted his only Son to the care of a human mother is proof enough that we potentially possess all the love and intelligence necessary for the raising of a child.

That some of us will have an easier time at it than others probably reflects attitudes. How do you see this period of your life? As an interruption—a time to get through quickly so that you can return to a more glamorous career? Or as a gift of joy and private satisfaction? And no matter how positively you may have entered into motherhood, attitudes continue to influence you—even to the point of determining the relationship you'll share with your child.

Motherhood holds many choices. You can become a cruel master, or an overworked slave —or you can guide and help your child to gradual independence. You can be respected like a good boss, or you can be feared as a mighty tyrant. You can cling possessively to your child until he becomes a social cripple, or you can let go daily as he broadens his boundaries. How will you know which direction to turn? By adopting the attitude of trust.

Trust God to help you raise your child.

I will instruct you (says the Lord) and guide you along the best pathway for your life; I will advise you and watch your progress (Psalm 32:8, TLB).

God wants you to be a mother. He placed you where you are for a certain reason, and he'll see you through. But beyond just seeing you through, he'll help you discover the blessings that motherhood evokes... the same blessings that the angel spoke of to the virgin Mary so long ago. Yes, blessed are thou among women—*you* are a mother.

A baby is is an inestimable burden and blessing.—Mark Twain

Appearance— a more glorious you

Funny, but the very women who so ardently monitor their lives during pregnancy are often the worst offenders of post-partum health care. Oh, I'm not talking about following the doctor's medical instructions, I'm speaking of simple body maintenance, for that in itself has a great deal to do with health.

We as Christian women should be particularly interested in taking care of ourselves, because we are more than mothers and wives and working people—we are living testimonies of our love for Christ.

For ye are bought with a price; therefore glorify God in your body, and in your spirit, which are God's (1 Corinthians 6:20).

Yet look around you in church next Sunday. Although you'll find many women glorifying God in spirit, you'll find a smaller number doing the same in body. What a shame.

When you were pregnant, your whole being was a manifestation of glory. Remember how beautiful you felt? Now that same "glory" may be a bit harder to come by, but you'll still want to make the effort. Praising God in body and in spirit is simply another aspect of being a mother, a wife, a woman, and a Christian.

During the first few weeks of motherhood, the simplest toiletry may seem an impossible feat. So, when you're down and out, and tempted to forego even the most basic beauty routine, take another glance at the following suggestions for quick inspiration.

EVERYDAY PRIORITIES

You, the mother, deserve the same sensible care that you gave yourself as the mother-to-be.
- a balanced diet
- plenty of sleep
- fresh air
- correction of physical disorders
- exercise

Beyond these basics, however, there are certain areas to which every well-groomed mother should give special attention.

SKIN CARE

Dry skin. What with all the hormonal changes taking place in your body, motherhood is apt to find your skin drier than usual. To relieve dry skin, try taking a daily oil bath, or follow your shower with a generous anointing of body lotion. Low on funds? A half cup of cornstarch added to the bath water is a fine substitute for oil.

Chapped hands. Now your hands are constantly in and out of water, rinsing diapers, preparing formula, or just keeping things clean. Station a bottle of hand cream beside each sink, and use it.

Stretch marks. Often called the badge of motherhood, striae never entirely disappear, but it's true that you can minimize them and help them to fade with the daily application of a cream or lotion designed for this purpose. Although you probably began using such a cream during pregnancy, many women would advise you to continue this practice until you've regained your pre-pregnancy figure. It's for you to decide.

Complexion. Again, due to hormone imbalance, your complexion may be temporarily dry or oily after the birth of a baby. Some women discover that cosmetics which were once just right are no longer suitable. When this happens, ask a beauty consultant to help you select the appropriate cleansing and moisturizing products. Do something nice for your complexion once in a while, like having a professional facial, or pampering yourself with a masque. The following recipes are ideal for just about all skin types.

The egg white masque. Beat the white of an egg. A dash of lemon for oily skin or a small amount of olive oil for dry skin may be added, but neither is necessary. Smooth the preparation on your face, avoiding the area around your eyes. Let it dry for fifteen minutes. Rinse with cool water.

The oatmeal masque. Prepare oatmeal as for eating. Let it cool, then smooth it on your face and neck. Let it dry for thirty minutes. Rinse with warm water.

14 APPEARANCE

APPEARANCE

HAIR CARE

Style. Suddenly there's no time for hairwashing. A short blow-dry cut has saved the day for many a mother, but if you're reluctant to part with those long tresses, perhaps a ponytail tied with a colorful ribbon would solve your new hair problem. Keep a bag of tricks up your sleeve—dry shampoo, an inexpensive wig, a collection of pretty scarves.

Falling hair. It's not uncommon for women to notice a large hair loss after pregnancy. Usually the hair resumes its normal growth pattern in a few months. But if this condition should cause you worry, consult your doctor. Hair breakage is another story, as it means that your hair has been damaged and can be treated. This, too, is a frequent complaint of new mothers. Permanents, straightening, coloring, teasing, wind, sun, salt water, and plain neglect all play a part in damaging hair. To remedy the situation, consider a hot oil treatment once a week, or one of the many instant treatments now available on the market. During this time, it might be wise to skip those nightly brushings, and to avoid the use of hair rollers whenever possible.

Homemade oil treatment. Apply one tablespoon of olive oil or castor oil to your scalp with a cotton ball. Massage into the scalp. Wrap your head in a hot towel and then step into a hot steamy bath or shower.

DENTAL HYGIENE

Because you must now move on quickly from meals to another important task, finding time or perhaps just remembering to brush your teeth can become a problem. Write yourself a note and tack it to the bathroom door—you'll soon be back in the habit. Keep up with your yearly dental checkup, for if you neglect your teeth now, chances are you'll be in line for extensive repair work about the same time that junior needs braces. And guess who comes first?

FOOT CARE

Proper foot care for the mother involves wearing comfortable shoes that fit well. Before slipping your feet into shoes, however, follow these simple guidelines:
1. Dry feet thoroughly after bathing.
2. Apply a moisturizing body lotion.
3. Dust with foot or talcum powder.

Remember, correcting physical disorders is one of your priorities. That means you'll put any feet problems such as ingrown toenails under the care of a doctor.

FRAGRANCE

Do use fragrance every day regardless of whether or not you'll be stepping out the front door. There's baby, hubby, and you—all three important enough to smell feminine for.

EXTRA HINTS

The beauty box. Sharing a bathroom with the family? Avoid the frustration of hunting for this and that, by preparing a beauty box to keep in the bedroom. This can be nothing more than a shoe box in which you keep a comb and brush, a razor, body lotion, deodorant, and simple makeup basics.

Sore muscle reliever. Stand under a shower, hot as you can tolerate it for about five minutes, or add a half cup of Epsom salt to the bath water.

For quick energy. Take an alternating hot and cold shower.

To cool off. Bathe in slightly cool, not cold, water. Dust yourself with bath powder.

Wardrobe saver. Keep your clothing fresh all day by wearing a smock when feeding or bathing baby. (One of hubby's old shirts will do nicely.)

A good mother doesn't have time to primp. But the woman who does practice body maintenance isn't living just to look beautiful—her "living" is beautiful.

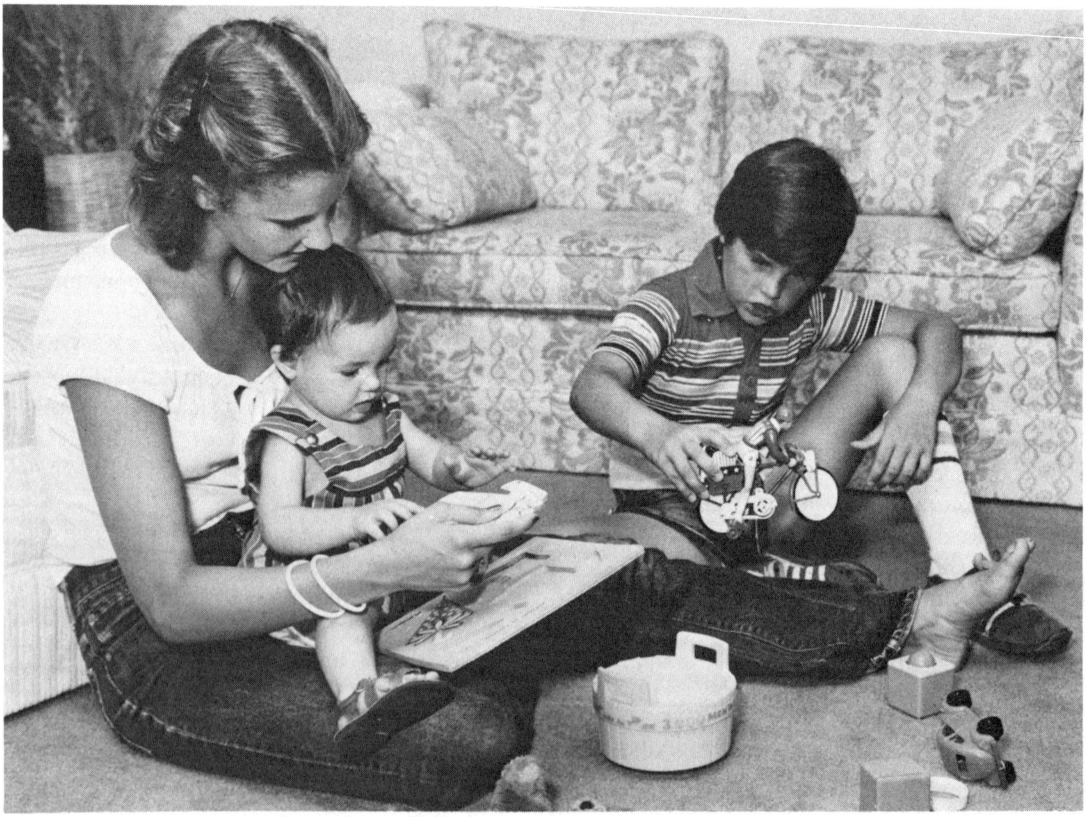

Baby-sitters—
how to have a baby-sitter and your peace of mind too

The evening had been splendid. My husband paid the baby-sitter, I checked in on our slumbering child, and together we collapse the bed in one exhausted heap. A perfect "night out." That is, almost.

The next morning, while getting dre' discovered that not only was most of her wardrobe gone, but a good sampling drugs articles such as earrings and prescrip' also seemed to have disappeared. And

"Impossible!" was my first thou, Sure then I remembered the baby-sitt/one other enough, our thief turned out to ! ger. It than Susie, the all-American te, n taken in by was painful to admit that we'd !out it was a girl several years our junio, ige that we'd even more painful to acknow

Instead, make it a practice to have your children dressed and ready for bed before you leave for the evening.

The baby-sitter is by nature a hungry creature, and I've known a few who wouldn't repeat the job if there wasn't something around the house to nibble on. This is a courtesy that you're obligated to render, so if you don't want your kitchen raided, leave a hearty snack on a tray with a note informing the baby-sitter that plans have already been made for the food in the refrigerator.

This is a good time to bring up the question of extra duties. It's probably best not to add extra responsibilities such as cleaning and ironing to the baby-sitter's job, not even for a bonus. You may have to ask her to feed the children once in awhile, but it's important to remember that any additional work will only keep her away from her first duty—the children.

Besides leaving the name and telephone number of the place where you can be reached, give the baby-sitter all the information she may need about you. Write your name, address, and the children's names on a piece of paper placed next to the telephone. And before saying, "goodbye," you'll need to set the rules of the house. It's perfectly all right to insist upon no telephone chats and no visitors. One good way to insure that your rules are followed is to warn the baby-sitter that although you should be home at a given time, you might call or even return unexpectedly.

If you come home to find your children asleep or playing happily, your house in the order you left it, and the baby-sitter quietly reading or watching television, you've found yourself a gem, and you'd best treat her with care. Give her the respect of always returning on time, pay her promptly and fairly, and compliment her on a job well done.

But if your children are unhappy, your home dismantled, and there are telltale signs of broken rules, this person is not for you. Baby-sitters are never as scarce as they sometimes seem. Co-ops, professional baby-sitters, and child care centers can be found in almost every community and may be your answer.

Of course, you'll hear the usual complaints from your brood the next day, for no baby-sitter's lap will ever be as soft as yours, and no baby-sitter will be able to read stories or even dry a tear the way you do. But that's all right, because the one thing you never want in a baby-sitter is someone to replace you, the mother.

Boredom— RX for the housewife blues

Symptoms: Chronic fatigue, absence of laughter, low self-esteem, frequent temptation to return to former career
Cause: Insufficient variety in daily activities
Treatment: Begin collecting God's promises
Eye hath not seen, nor ear heard, neither have entered into the heart of man, the things which God hath prepared for them that love him (1 Corinthians 2:9).

So you're a housewife now. No doubt you chose this role deliberately and of your own free will. You wanted to create a comfortable resting place for your husband after a hard day's work; a nest for your little ones to reach maturity in—and you've given it your best. But somehow you hadn't expected the boredom that comes from a day of wiping runny noses and washing dishes. None of us do. After all, we've spent almost our entire lives in a highly structured environment, first the classroom and then the office. We know nothing of organizing time and developing achievements. Even so, it doesn't take long to discover that there's got to be more to life than routine.

One woman refers to this "more" as soul-feeding. It's the extra that makes your day special regardless of how many mundane

Baby-sitters— how to have a baby-sitter and your peace of mind too

The evening had been splendid. My husband paid the baby-sitter, I checked in on our slumbering child, and together we collapsed on the bed in one exhausted heap. A perfect "night out." That is, almost.

The next morning, while getting dressed, I discovered that not only was most of my wardrobe gone, but a good sampling of other articles such as earrings and prescription drugs also seemed to have disappeared.

"Impossible!" was my first thought. And then I remembered the baby-sitter. Sure enough, our thief turned out to be none other than Susie, the all-American teenager. It was painful to admit that we'd been taken in by a girl several years our junior, but it was even more painful to acknowledge that we'd made a poor judgment at the expense of our own daughter.

"Wow," my best friend commented after hearing my tale of woe. "What bad luck."

Luck? I wish it had been merely a matter of luck. Whether my friend knew it or not, this was one unfortunate experience that could have been avoided with a little foresight, and a slightly different approach.

He that handleth a matter wisely shall find good: and whoso trusteth in the Lord, happy is he (Proverbs 16:20).

Perhaps the best question to ask is: how often do we show wisdom in arranging for child care? It all begins with the choice of a baby-sitter. Where do you find one? Well, Susie had come to *us*, and although there are many sincere people out there, it's probably best to avoid the baby-sitter who advertises, unless her references are outstanding. And even then, they should be carefully checked.

Parents seeking a good baby-sitter usually rely upon recommendations from each other, the daughters of well-thought-of neighbors, and sometimes the help of a church secretary who knows her congregation.

The age of a dependable baby-sitter varies widely; but do keep in mind that maturity comes at a different time for everyone, and has little to do with physical appearance. If the person you are considering seems to like children, talks intelligently to you over the phone, and is reasonably priced, you're at least on the right track.

One friend of mine always invites a new baby-sitter over for a get-acquainted session before she actually hires her. "Could you come over for about thirty minutes to meet my children and see if you might be interested in baby-sitting?" is the way she tactfully puts it.

This is a marvelous chance to observe not only the maturity of the girl, but her speech, mode of dress, and attitude toward children. The everyday values of your household should always be upheld in your selection of a baby-sitter, because when you hire her, you are in a way saying, "This is someone I think highly of."

After you've chosen your baby-sitter, perhaps the first time you'd like her to sit for you during the day for an hour or two. Arrange transportation details, then ask her to be available about twenty minutes early so that you can show her around the house and still have time to leave proper instructions.

As you show her through the house, be clear as to which rooms she and the children may have access to. If guard gates are providing safety boundaries for small children, emphasize their purpose. Point out the heater and air-conditioner controls and explain how to regulate the room temperature. It's generally assumed that the baby-sitter may watch television or listen to the stereo, so save yourself a repair bill, and show her how this equipment works.

Sometimes parents forget how unique their children's various routines are, but there are certain things about every child that a baby-sitter should never be left to guess. For instance, let the baby-sitter know each child's toilet procedure. If the child is still learning, you might leave an ample supply of training pants with instructions to simply keep him dry. But if he merely needs an occasional reminder, you'll want to write his potty times down on a piece of paper along with a note of when, where, and what he may eat and drink.

For some reason, parents are quick to mention bedtimes, but often forget to let the baby-sitter in on those all-important bedtime comforts such as special blankets, toys, nightlights, and window shades. And even though you'll show her where to find diapers and fresh clothing, never ask the baby-sitter to give baths. The bathtub holds so many accident possibilities that it's really not fair for you to thrust this responsibility upon her.

chores you've done in between. In the office, it's being given a new responsibility or having lunch with an old school chum. At home it's slipping sachet into the folds of the linens or polishing the brass bed until it sparkles.

God doesn't want our lives to be dismal. The Bible tells us that there are many exciting "extras" in store for those who love Christ. But finding those extras in the dirty clothes hamper is a challenge, indeed, and may even call for a little prompting.

If you'd like to start collecting some of the fascinating everyday experiences that God is saving for you, but don't know where to begin, why not try establishing a Happiness Calendar? It's really a very simple idea: at the beginning of each month you will write down one special activity for each day of that month. These ideas can be as elaborate or as simple as your time permits, but they should never hinder you from preparing a good dinner or tending to your children's needs.

Need some help to get your first month going?

1. Make a rag doll. Cloth dolls have strong appeal to both boys and girls, and have a strange habit of capturing the heart of their creator as well.
2. Bake bread. Find a good bread recipe and let this cooking adventure become a regular part of your week.
3. Visit the library, and check out art and photography books. They'll satisfy your craving to hold a book without demanding reading time.
4. Give yourself a facial.
5. Work on your children's memory books. Heights, weights, and special accomplishments might not be remembered in a few years.
6. Invent your own main dish recipes.
7. Watch television unabashedly for hours on end.
8. Call a friend whom you seldom get to chat with.
9. Prepare a surprise candlelight dinner for your family.
10. Invite a friend to lunch.
11. Make cookies and head for the drive-in movies (if hubby's willing, of course).
12. Feed the ducks at your local pond.
13. Pick wild weeds. Then spray them with gold spray paint for a lovely inexpensive arrangement.
14. Select and send through the mail a zany card of love to your husband.
15. Start a kitchen herb garden.
16. Prepare menus for a month in advance.
17. Clean out a closet or drawer that's full of beloved junk.
18. Dress your children up for one of the special inexpensive portraits that many department stores now offer.
19. Make yourself a colorful tunic, using one of the easy-sew patterns.
20. Rearrange your spice cabinet, ending with a cup of spiced tea.
21. Make a homemade bath relaxer (two parts soda to one part salt) and take a midday bath.
22. Go to a garage sale. Look for old books, baby clothes, and maternity clothes.
23. Give yourself an old-fashioned hot-oil hair treatment.
24. Start a family bulletin board.
25. Polish your furniture with lemon oil.
26. Hunt through magazines for free booklet offers. Send off the request forms and wait for your mailbox to fill up with interesting mail.
27. Visit a new park with your children.
28. Collect and organize coupons for grocery shopping.
29. Rearrange your children's bedrooms. Children love the idea of an almost new room.
30. Write a letter to someone who might get only bills this month.
31. Have a "very merry un-birthday" party complete with cake, decorations, and a small gift for each member of the family.

Church—
the hallelujah hassle

There are some women who can make it on time for church and look beautiful in spite of having wrestled with children to get ready. And then there are others of us for whom "being on time" or "looking beautiful" is not even the issue, for we can't seem to make it to church, period. When we do manage to sneak into a back pew at the last minute, all windblown and wrinkled, most of us are so fatigued from the getting there, that we do well to stay awake.

That's when mothers begin asking themselves, "Why am I bothering?" And the more we ask the question, the more likely we are to roll over for another hour of sleep when the alarm goes off on Sunday morning.

Friends are sympathetic. "Church isn't really important," they'll say. "It's how you feel inside that counts." But don't be deceived, because it isn't just your imagination that life goes better when we attend church. It's stark reality. And it works that way because church is a part of Christian living.

"Why?" asked one woman. "God is everywhere—not just in your fancy chapel."

Maybe you can already answer this woman's question. Or perhaps you've never really answered it for yourself. Whatever the situation, one fact remains the same. Understanding our motivation for church attendance is a strong weapon against backsliding in the Christian life.

A friend once told me that she went to church because it was her only chance for peace and quiet in a family of four children. While this is certainly not a very lofty reason for attending church—how true it is. And when you think about it, what better way to escape the jingle-jangle of household music than to sit in the quietness of God's house?

Mothers need to make the most of this weekly appointment with inner solitude. We can leave our babies and small children in the nursery. We can enter the sanctuary in prayerful attitude. And we can sit patiently during the organ prelude and listen for God's voice.

This is the time to reflect back on our week. Are there any troubles that need to be laid at our Lord's feet? Any confessions of greed or selfishness? All of this, you see, is one reason we go to church. It gives us the opportunity to meet God in the proper setting, and with the best of advantages. When people claim to come away from a church service without having worshiped, it's usually their own fault; this is the one time and place where there should be nothing else to do but walk hand in hand with God.

Church is a place of Christian fellowship. Not just the social fellowship we share with other Christians, but the fellowship of prayer and praise, as well. It's comforting to hear our prayers offered up in great numbers, and it's pure joy to sing of God's glory in unison with others.

Sometimes people say, "I would go to church, but what's the use—everyone there acts like a heathen." And I too have experienced disappointments in Christian character. But the church is made up of human beings who recognize their need for God. Man is not perfect, and so the organized church of today will never be free of blemish. There is, however, no other place that can offer us the same strength we gain from joining other people who seek God's presence in the church. Christian fellowship, then, is another reason for making an all-out effort toward Sunday worship.

Others of us go to church to stock up on love. It takes so much of this precious ingredient to raise a family and live with our fellowman that sometimes by the end of the week, we find ourselves running short. Sibling rivalry, marital squabbles, neighborhood feuds—how on earth can women handle these everyday crises when their own wells are dry? So off to church we go each Sunday, happy to throw away the outer trappings of life in exchange for the love of God.

Experiencing the grace of God gives us the courage to reach out and actually pull it to ourselves, so that others whom we see during the week may know of this wonderful grace and love. There is a kind of urgency for mothers to grow as Christians. We know that we must, for we are a spiritual temple. Our lives are the pathway to salvation for our children, our friends, and in some instances, our husbands. That worn "dishpan-red" hand may well be the one that someone in need reaches out for. Can we afford to be less than full of God's love?

Christians strive for Christlikeness. Going to church and studying the Scriptures were both practiced by Christ. We, too, hunger for new knowledge of the Bible.

And he came to Nazareth, where he had been brought up; and, as his custom was, he went into the synagogue on the sabbath day, and stood up for to read (Luke 4:16).

But most of all we go to church because we love Christ. The Bible tells us that the church is the very body of Christ.

For no man ever yet hated his own flesh; but nourisheth and cherisheth it, even as the Lord the church: For we are members of his body, of his flesh, and of his bones (Ephesians 5:29, 30).

And again in Colossians:

And he is the head of the body, the church... (Colossians 1:18a).

Nevertheless, going to church is an ordinary headache for mothers. Take a hint from my own mother, wife of a minister, and mom of five kids—be prepared. Use Saturday to polish shoes, wash heads, and press clothes. Go to bed early, and wake up determined. Setting the alarm an hour ahead of your usual rising time will keep you from being rushed. Serve a simple but sustaining breakfast—two hours of worship can be a long time for little stomachs. (Cheese on toast and orange juice is a favorite at our house.) And never be guilty of Sunday morning housecleaning; making beds and straightening the living area is rarely worth the tension it creates when done in a hurry. These hints don't guarantee easy success, but they should help you get to church, even if a little late.

Finally, my brethren, rejoice in the Lord (Philippians 3:1).

And perhaps I should add—it's a well-earned privilege.

Colic— temperamental tears

Ellen settled baby Tommy against her shoulder and began to rock. Back and forth, back and forth, the rhythm of the rocker filled the room with unyielding determination—but still Tommy cried.

"I just can't figure out what's the matter," the weary mother complained to her doctor the next morning. "He's not hungry, he's not wet, and he's not just lonely. Nothing I do seems to help. I've walked the floors with him, bounced him across my knees, rocked him, sung to him, and talked to him, but it's no use. Maybe I just wasn't cut out for this motherhood bit."

Dr. Simmons listened sympathetically while examining the fretful infant. In a few minutes he looked up and announced, "Colic."

Ellen felt strangely weak. She was remembering what she knew about colic—those old wives' tales that point accusingly at Mom. If there was anything in the world she couldn't cope with just now, this was it. The room began echoing with sobs, only this time it wasn't Tommy. Dr. Simmons sighed—he'd seen it all many times before.

Tommy is not unique. Babies come into this world crying. They cry for food, for warmth, for comfort, and for love, but it's when the crying goes beyond these things that mothers become worried and begin consulting professionals. In the case of colic, we usually have a pretty good idea of the diagnosis long before calling our doctor. The hard persistent cry, accompanied by the drawing up of legs and a distended abdomen, fits the baby book's description of this malady to a tee. Perhaps the baby passes a great deal of gas and seems to have these spells of crying only at a certain time of the day. But there are some babies who cry either with colic or just plain irritableness from morning till night, and these little critters can really baffle us parents.

Doctor Benjamin Spock reminds us that colic lasts about three months, is fairly common, and doesn't seem to do the baby any harm. "On the contrary," he says, "it occurs most often in babies that are developing and growing well."

Just knowing these facts may erase some of the tension in your household. But in the meantime, your baby is crying—what can you do about that?

The first thing you should do when you suspect that your baby has colic, is to get in touch with your doctor. Not because the colic is cause for alarm, but because you *will* be alarmed, and it never hurts to be absolutely sure when it comes to your child's health. Besides, the doctor may be able to give your baby relief with a mild medication. I say may, because there are many mothers who can attest to cases in which medication didn't seem to help. Should this happen to your baby, let the doctor know, as a change in the dosage or a different drug entirely might be in order.

If you'd like a sedative for your baby, but your doctor doesn't believe in them, find a doctor who thinks more along your lines. If you've tried everything but sedatives because *you* don't believe in them, you'll be digging pretty deep for resourceful ideas. But other women who have gone this route will assure you that you'll live through it all.

There's something about colic that makes a mother feel terribly insecure in her new role, and it's not uncommon to spend every waking hour examining yourself, wondering where you went wrong. Relax, no one went "wrong." The truth is, we really don't know what causes colic. Some experts say that colic often occurs in babies with a family history of eczema, hay fever, asthma, or other allergic disorders. So some mothers, thinking their baby is allergic to cow's milk, take this as a cue to begin a three-month regime of formula switching.

And then there's the theory that colic is brought upon by nervous mothers. While it's true that most mothers with colicky babies are nervous, let's be honest—who wouldn't be nervous after listening to the cry of a helpless infant for hours on end? Finally, the most frequently given reason for colic today is an immature digestive system. This may not mean much to you and me, but it goes a long way when Grandma or the nosy neighbor wants to know what's wrong with your baby.

Baby's first three months will go by fast. During that time, your little one will grow and change so much that in your excitement over his accomplishments you might not even notice that he no longer has the ol' tummy ache. It may be even longer before you realize that you've grown and changed a great deal, too. Suddenly, you discover that patience is now one of your virtues, a messy house no longer depresses you, and even more wonderful, you can sew, eat a gourmet dinner, or carry on a conversation, all in between the demands of motherhood. Congratulations, you have arrived. But to make it easier along the way, how about a few pointers?

1. Develop a mental check list. Is your baby hungry? wet? cold? lonely? sleepy? just plain fretful? Only after you've reached the end of your list are you ready to administer medication prescribed for colic.

2. Give the baby his medication, play with him for a few minutes, and then lay him on his tummy in his bed. Babies with colic are usually more comfortable on their stomachs,

> Trust in the Lord with all thine heart; and lean not unto thine own understanding (Proverbs 3:5).

and this procedure often works best for helping the baby fall asleep. But if your baby stops crying only when you're holding him, by all means, hold him. You'll both feel happier.

3. In between medication dosages, try a pacifier, walking, rocking, riding in the car, or a warm hot water bottle placed on the baby's tummy. Please do check the heat of the bottle, making sure that you can comfortably rest it against your wrist, and wrap it in a diaper.

4. Offer frequent small feedings instead of trying to stick to a schedule, always remembering to burp a baby afterward.

5. If your baby seems to be at his worst when you leave the house, avoid large crowds and drafty places. Some mothers have found that in extreme cases of colic it works best not to even take the baby outside for as long as the colic persists.

6. Make sure that the baby is always comfortably warm. Some colicky babies like to be swaddled in receiving blankets most of the time.

7. The end of the day will probably find you exhausted. Make an arrangement with your husband in which you'll take turns napping during those most difficult hours.

8. Never give the baby any medication not prescribed for him by your doctor.

9. Make an effort to relax. Put the relaxation exercises that you learned in your childbirth classes into practice again, fix yourself a refreshing beverage, and rest your feet.

10. Remember to rely upon the Lord. He can give you the strength and courage necessary to meet each day with renewed spirit.

We know that both bottle and breastfed infants can have colic, but if you're nursing, you deserve special encouragement. A colicky baby doesn't always sleep well, and you're going to feel tired and run-down. In order to get as much rest as possible, you'll probably discover that it's mandatory to curtail all but the most basic activities.

If household help is out of the question, let the house go, with the knowledge that in a few months there'll be more than enough time to scrub and clean.

Join a nursing organization for moral support, but don't let the energy of other mothers discourage you. Yours is a special situation that even with its hardships has its blessing. You'll always have plenty of milk because colicky babies are enthusiastic nursers.

Above all, don't quit nursing just because of colic. Your baby needs the warmth of your arms, the smell of your body; and you, yourself, can benefit from the calm that comes with the letdown of milk.

No one's going to tell you that a colicky baby is all fun and games, but the mother who patiently dedicates this period of her life to her baby will find that she gains maturity as a mother and wisdom as a woman—not a bad bonus to receive from any job.

> As seen on the wall in a church nursery:
> "We shall not all sleep, but we shall all be changed"
> (1 Corinthians 15:51).

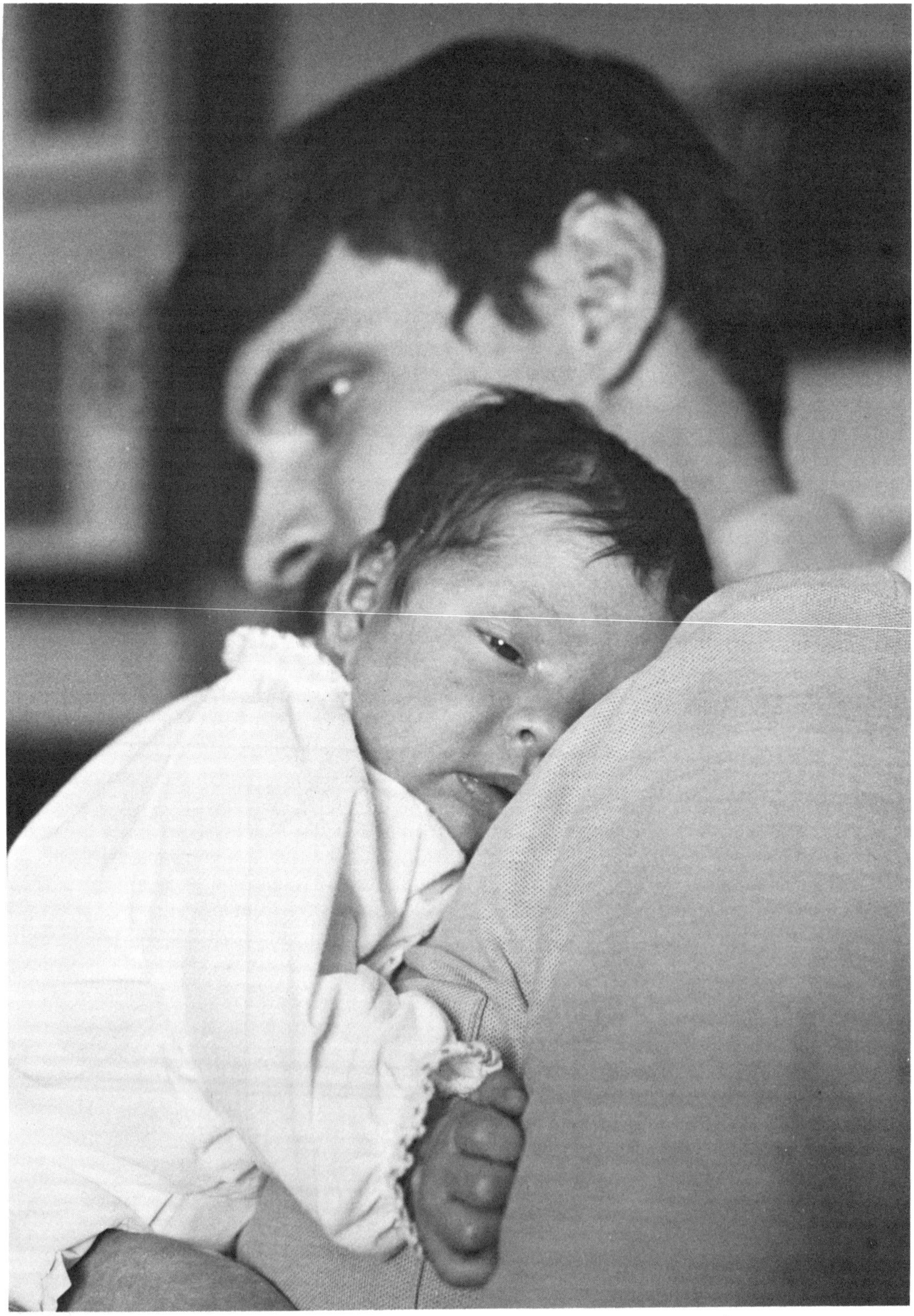

Dads—
when proud papa becomes a passive father

"I'd really like for the kids to get to know their father, but with him coming home after their bedtime every night, there's not much of a chance for that," the young mother complained.

"It's the same at our house," spoke up another.

"And at ours," said still another.

The scene was a neighborhood coffee klatch, and the conversation was taking a familiar turn. "Why are some men such terrific fathers while others remain practically indifferent?" these women wanted to know. As I listened to their exchange of ideas, I could remember asking myself the same question not so very long ago.

A lot seems to be stacked against fatherhood today. Our men are so busy. They're either holding down two jobs in order to meet the rising cost of living, or they're traveling to meet sales quotas. And those who do have some spare time always seem to be weekend golfers, or just too old-fashioned to discard the belief that child care is woman's work. Where, oh where are the liberated men that we read about in magazines? The ones that wash dishes, cook, and diaper the baby because it's "their thing"?

Christian women are right to be concerned about the father's role in the home. The love between father and child is an important relationship to be established in your family. We can see just how important it is by turning to the Bible, for here, the father/son relationship is used over and over again to illustrate the relationship between Christ and man.

Behold, what manner of love the Father hath bestowed upon us, that we should be called the sons of God (1 John 3:1a).

Regardless of its importance, a wife won't have much luck at forcing the duty of fathering upon her husband. Yet, because she's the homemaker, it's in her department. Just as she wouldn't neglect a torn curtain or soiled carpet, she won't neglect family ties that need mending or building. It may not be possible or even advisable to convince a husband that fathering is masculine or to persuade him to give up a second job, traveling for business, or weekend golf. It is possible, however, to be a real dad no matter the life style. Like mothering, fathering doesn't necessarily come naturally. But while women can pick up trade secrets from friends, relatives, and books written especially for them, men have few resources to turn to. That's where you, the mother, come in.

Consider pregnancy to be the beginning of your family life. If this is your first baby, you'll soon find yourself trying to remember what it was like before the two of you became parents, so you need this nine months of waiting as a final farewell to the "couple's" life.

But even experienced parents will discover that each new baby brings changes to their family life. Entertain, go out as often as you feel up to it, and sleep late on Saturdays, for these are the things you'll yearn for most during those early years of motherhood. At the same time, however, begin gradually breaking away from the idea of a twosome world. Spend lazy afternoons in planning. Decide together when you'll announce your pregnancy, what you'll name the baby, where the baby will be born, and where he'll sleep once home. Walk together each day and let your thoughts wander toward the future. Talk about the layette, the nursery, and all the baby equipment you'll need. Then when it's time to shop, go together. Browse through garage sales and antique shops for that one truly unique item.

Learn together. Place child care books in strategic spots around the house. A friend of mine suggests the bathroom, and I have to admit it's not a bad idea. Attend not only childbirth education classes, but baby care classes as well. These classes teach prospective parents how to cope with pregnancy and how to care for baby after he arrives. Plan on a cooperative delivery with dad not just present, but helping. And top it all off with rooming-in. Since you're actually responsible for some of the baby's care in this situation, it provides a wonderful opportunity for breaking a father into diapering and feeding.

Next stop—home. More than likely, the bottlefeeding mother has got an enthusiastic volunteer to take over night-time feedings, and the breastfeeding mother has probably promised every burping to Dad. Together you can bathe the baby before bedtime and rock him during those short spurts of wakefulness. But whether it's colic or just ordinary boredom, something usually happens to help wear off the newness of baby and all at once you find it's no longer fun. Quite often, the father of a nursing baby begins to feel left out and takes up a new hobby, or the father who once so eagerly fed the evening bottle stops coming home in time to help with this activity. "Jim used to be so crazy about the baby; now he completely ignores her," cried one woman.

This is the time to remember that fathering is learned. Be patient and loving, and Papa is sure to fit into the mold sometime during the first year. But since it is important for father and child to develop strong feelings from the beginning, you'll want to find ways to unobtrusively slip fathering into your husband's life. Here are a few suggestions.

1. Arrange for your husband to entertain the baby while you bathe each night.
2. Start the custom of father and child dinners. Dad feeds the baby while drinking a glass of iced tea and munching on cheese. Where are you? Fixing dinner, of course.
3. Plan for your husband to bathe the baby once a week.
4. Whenever possible, let Dad accompany you, or go in your place, on your baby's visits to the doctor.
5. Let your husband select and purchase some of the baby's clothing.
6. Encourage a quiet time between father and child before bedtime. This can begin with rocking and grow into bedtime reading.

Relax and give your husband freedom when it comes to your child. In other words, be careful about giving advice. Of course, you do things differently, and yes, maybe even better. But let your husband have the privilege of doing things his way. Occasionally, you may feel inclined to ask him for *his* opinion on various matters, but don't depend on Hubby to make up your mind about everyday matters.

As you watch your husband and child become friends, you'll notice that even a baby senses the specialness of Dad. My daughter learned to pull up, clap her hands, walk, and many other things from her father—not from me. And with such rapport, is it any wonder that a baby's first word is usually "Da-da"?

Because Dad's not around as much as you, his patience may be greater. In fact, in his book, *How to Father*, Dr. Fitzhugh Dodson advises us to *let* Dad deal with all the minor mishaps that come as a result of baby's antics. And since Dad has nerves of steel, let him teach baby those skills that require one or two knots on the head along the way to mastery.

Some women are so successful in turning their husbands into fathers that they begin to feel left out themselves. Never allow yourself to feel this way. That child is an extension of you—your gift to your husband. His total acceptance and absolute love for your gift is one of the many ways of saying, "I love you." And isn't that what being a parent is all about anyway?

Discipline— setting the stage for discipline

All of life is a stage. It was Shakespeare who coined the phrase, and it's true. For life is indeed a drama—with birth, death, happiness, and sadness all taking place on center stage. And how important that stage is to life's actors. Why, the proper lighting, setting, and instructions can quite literally spell success or failure in later years.

So, when parents begin blocking the action for their children's lives, the matter of discipline invariably comes up. Unfortunately, a lot of us are afraid of discipline. We associate it with harsh punishments and unhappy memories of childhood. Some of us are not even sure what discipline means, but since it sounds so complicated and involved, we're likely to ignore it entirely. Still others think that a psychology degree with an elaborate "clinical" vocabulary stands for instant expertise.

Directors wouldn't think of approaching a play without understanding. Likewise, those of us directing human lives shouldn't depend on neighborhood advice and threadbare memories when it comes to the subject of discipline. Read about it, study it, and decide for yourself what type of discipline will best suit your life style. Consider the following notes and make some of your own. Then, and only then, are you ready to direct your cast.

DIRECTOR'S NOTE—
throw more light on discipline.

First of all, strike the notion that discipline is punishment. Think of it as teaching and training. Training that's necessary in order to live happily and safely in our society. But not the kind of training that we would give to a pet. Pets need only learn commands, while children must learn to think and act on their own. School teachers tell us that their best teaching results come when they give guidance and place control on their pupils, but then stand aside so that learning can take place. This is in essence what parents are doing when they set boundaries and limits, and take a stand on issues that children can't handle. Children need this guidance. They can't cope with complete freedom, although even an eighteen-month-old baby will do his best to convince you he's capable.

DIRECTOR'S NOTE—use backdrop of love.

Where does discipline begin? With birth. It's part of that first love you feel for your little one. Cultivate that love and make sure it grows, for we as humans have a tendency to want to obey and learn from those we love. Christians know this from experience—we love God and we strive to obey him and adopt his ways.

As for the learning that begins at birth, it's so subtle that sometimes we're not even aware it's going on. But it is, for the tiny baby learns from his parents that a bed is for sleeping, the highchair is for eating, the bathtub for bathing, and the car seat for outings. Because he isn't allowed to sleep in the bathtub and eat in his bed, the baby is slowly learning the basics of living in society. Please remember that you can't spoil a baby. To allow a baby to cry from hunger, wetness, or boredom isn't discipline—it's cruelty.

Most of us begin to think seriously on discipline when baby begins to crawl. We're not sure if we should slap his hand and say "no" to treasure hunting, or simply put the treasures out of reach. You have to do what you feel best. But be aware that if you do lean toward hand slapping, it won't guarantee the safety of priceless keepsakes. And then there's baby's safety. When he decides to crawl, you'll need every break you can get, for a lot of damage can be done in that moment your back is turned. Don't take chances:

Put poisons away and latch-hook all cabinet doors.

Cover electrical sockets with plates purchased at hardware stores, or cover with heavy furniture.

Put away breakable and heavy objects that could be pulled off tables.

Survey the house for unusual items of danger, such as sewing equipment and tools.

DIRECTOR'S NOTE—
move downstage with ideas.

Spankings? Well, certainly not for anyone under the age of two. Distraction is a handy device in baby discipline. Nature makes this form of discipline instinctive up to a point. Baby grabs the diaper pin, and without even thinking, Mom exchanges the pin for powder. Apply the same techniques with your older baby. Exchange those forbidden objects for something of equal intrigue—a tape measure, a pretty ribbon, or an old dress pattern that he can crinkle and tear.

Rewards are another way to teach the young child or toddler who is beginning to learn right from wrong. Baby plays quietly during nap time, even though he thinks he's getting too big for a rest period, and you reward him with a small surprise and the remark, "Because you were so good." Of course, teaching by example is also an effective discipline method. And it's easy because you simply treat your baby with the same courtesy and respect that you'll expect from him someday. Knock on his bedroom door before entering, and use "please" and "excuse me" in your speech.

But you'll probably find the reinforcement of praise and love to be your most effective disciplining tool. I remember that my own mother would always tell us kids how nice we looked, and how proud of our manners she was. It made us feel so wonderful, that we'd practically burst our seams trying to be good. So praise your baby for goodness even when it's bound to be "accidental" on his part. Good children are so often ignored, it's no wonder we don't seem to see many.

DIRECTOR'S NOTE—redo last scene.

There'll be times when you miss the mark completely. When what you thought was best, simply wasn't. Admit your mistake and apologize. Once after scolding my daughter for picking up what I assumed to be a cigarette butt, I discovered she had merely been clutching a piece of candy. Our friend laughed when I said, "I'm sorry," but Heather didn't. She might have only been a baby, but she was still a person. And because I admitted my wrong, she regained her dignity and her faith in me.

DIRECTOR'S NOTE—curtain call.

There's not really an alternative to discipline. Either you do or you don't. But when you get down to the nitty-gritty, there's not really a choice as to whether you do or you don't. Discipline is a parent's responsibility. All those rude, aggressive, uncontrolled children out there are a product of parents' overpermissiveness.

Train up a child in the way he should go: and when he is old, he will not depart from it (Proverbs 22:6).

Old advice? Well, maybe. Still, a lot of people are following it, even today. You can spot them easily in any crowd—they're the ones whose children portray "life" without the trauma of stage fright.

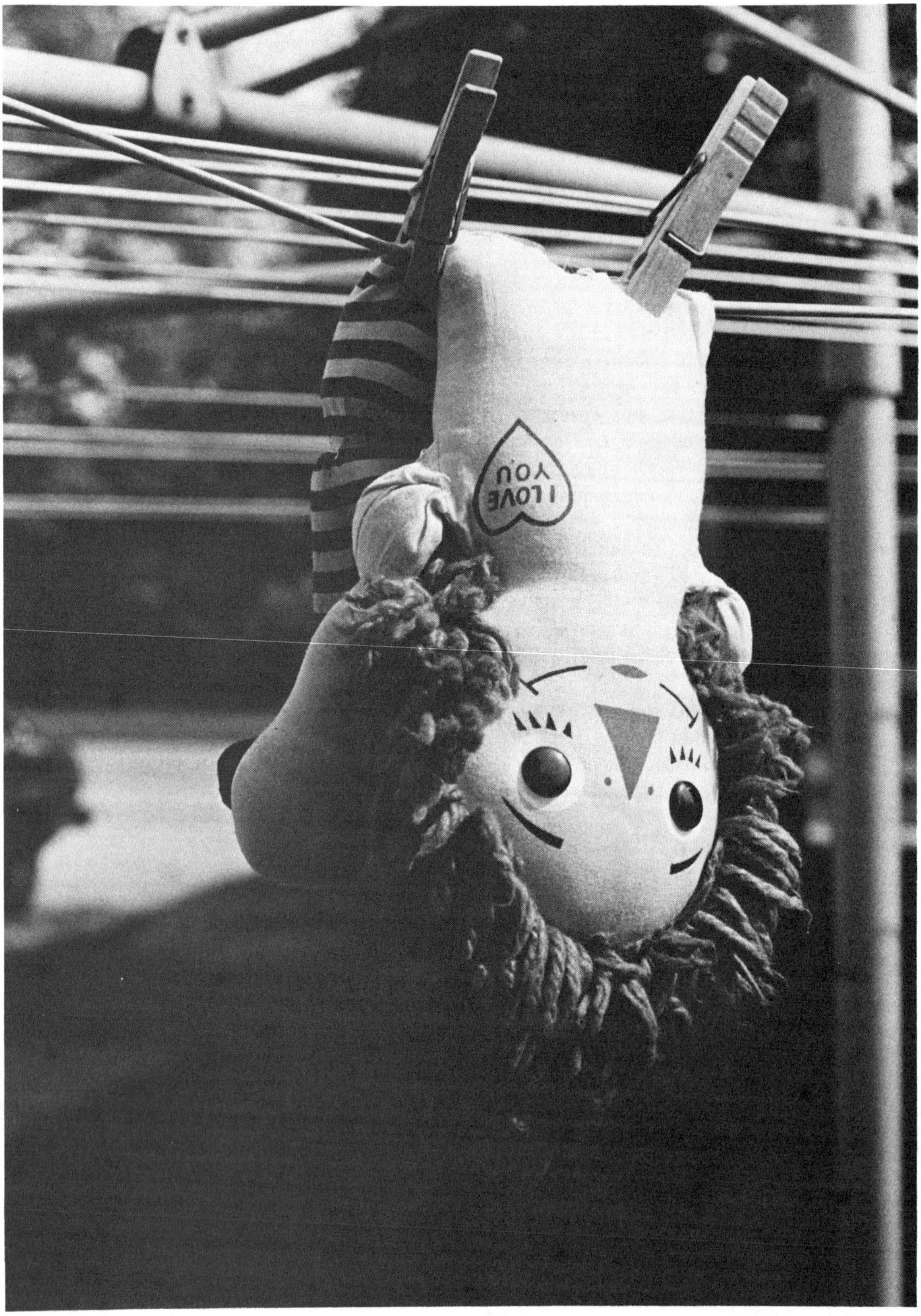
I LOVE
YOU

Emergencies—household SOS

I used to think the word emergency was synonymous with blood—without one you couldn't have the other. That, of course, was before I became a mother. For I have since learned that an emergency can be anything from a swallowed fish bone to an unexpected dinner guest.

Organized mothers readily admit to having some kind of an emergency plan behind every successful venture. These substitute plans are simple measures that any woman, given a little experience, could easily come up with. In fact, you may already be employing some of these tactics right now. Why not find out just how emergency-proof your household is by playing the following game?

You have only to answer the questions, adding or subtracting points as indicated. Do be honest with yourself—low scorers can try again next month for a perfect mark.

1. Baby burns himself on your curling iron. (Whoops, it shouldn't have been left unattended in the first place.) Give yourself 1 point for having a first-aid kit with the following items:
- first-aid manual
- scissors
- adhesive tape
- bandage strips
- sterile gauze bandage
- sterile gauze pads
- rubbing alcohol
- cream antiseptic
- thermometer
- antiseptic swab
- ice bag
- hot water bottle
- aspirin or equivalent
- boric acid eyewash

Subtract 1 point if you weren't sure where to look for your kit.

Add 1 point if it's been less than five years since you last read the first-aid manual. You might want to make it a practice to review emergency accident procedures once a year.

2. Old friends arrive in time for supper. Win 1 point by having an emergency menu plan.

SPUR-OF-THE-MOMENT MENUS

When there's no time to shop, rely on staples. Try to keep your pantry well stocked with eggs, biscuit mix, and canned luncheon meat at all times.
Serve:
- omelet
- biscuits
- bacon or fried luncheon meat
- popcorn for dessert

When shopping's no problem, but time is of the essence, take advantage of canned and frozen foods.
Serve:
- canned ravioli garnished with melted cheese and black olives
- tossed green salad
- brown-and-serve rolls
- frozen pie, cake, or turnovers for dessert

3. You've just received rather short notice of a birthday, shower, or anniversary. Add 2 points for ingenuity if you'd give any of the gifts below.
- a book from your paperback collection
- a cutting from a plant
- a promissory note
- any dearly loved possession of your own

4. Deduct 5 points if you don't carry a fully equipped diaper bag on all outings that include baby. A diaper tote should hold these basics: clean diapers and disposable wash-ups, powder or lotion, a change of clothing, and a snack.

5. Baby spits up on your best dress. Add 1 point if you keep a pinch of soda in your purse. (It'll remove that sour smell.) Sprinkle the soiled area with soda, rub gently with dampened cloth.

6. The water pipes are shut off unexpectedly; 5 points go to the mother who always keeps a full kettle of water on the stove.

7. It's Saturday night and the television's on the blink. Retrieve low spirits and earn 2 points by popping popcorn and declaring it game night.

8. An electrical storm leaves you in the dark. Deduct 1 point if you don't have a flashlight and candle in the house. Next Christmas might be a good time to splurge on a huge candle which you can use throughout the year for dinners and emergencies.

9. Thanksgiving dinner for twenty people, and the oven fails to heat; 4 points are coming your way if you'd:
    Inquire as to whether you could rent the church's kitchen.
    Suggest turkey dinner at the nearest cafeteria.

10. Both you and your husband have come down with a virus. A quicker recovery and 2 points are yours for arranging child care for the baby. Ask relatives, neighbors, or fellow church members to help locate a baby-sitter.

TALLYING YOUR SCORE:

A score between 18 and 20 means you think pretty fast and are adaptable besides.

A score between 10 and 15 indicates you're good ol' average Mom. The only person who really expects more from you is you yourself. Don't worry if you make a wrong move now and then; Hubby and Baby adore you for trying so hard.

Score under 8 suggests a rather hectic household. Perhaps Mom lacks the confidence to make emergency decisions, and so she simply doesn't. A lot of us face this difficulty in the early years of our marriage. It may help to remember, however, that a husband likes to think that his delicate, feminine wife who leans on him for her very life, can take charge in an emergency. And no matter how impossible it sounds, we know we can do just that because of a promise made long ago.

Lo, I am with you alway, even unto the end of the world (Matthew 28:20b).

So, we're never completely on our own, no matter what the emergency. What wonderful first-aid for a mother to carry in her heart.

Everyday things—bathing, diapering, and bedding your baby

Karen and I were pregnant at the same time. We visited each other often—comparing weight, baby gifts, maternity fashions, and sometimes fears. One of the things we both dreaded was bathing our babies. How could we ever bathe a piece of wiggly pink flesh? We talked, we read, and we watched other mothers bathing their babies. But when Karen gave birth a few weeks before me, she said, "Jayne, it's just as bad as we thought—I almost dropped Jenny during her morning bath."

Then my own daughter was born, and I was in for a pleasant surprise. Bathing a baby, I discovered, was neither very easy nor very difficult. It reminded me of driving a car; the more I did it, the more confident I became. But as with driving a car, being confident didn't give me the right to let up on safety, and I was glad I had talked and read and observed all that I could on the matter.

You, too, may be a bit shaky about your baby's first bath. So, perhaps a thorough understanding of the "typical" baby bath will make you more comfortable. But when you do take off on your own, remember that as in other areas of infant care, when it comes to bathing a baby, your common sense is the real authority.

BATHING

Equipment. Try using a bath basket to keep the baby's bath needs all together. This can be a pretty wicker basket decorated with ribbons, an ordinary utility tray, or anything that has a handle and can be easily carried from nursery to bathing area. Your basket should hold a bar of mild soap and soap dish, cotton balls, cotton swabs, baby oil, lotion and powder, a soft wash cloth and towel, and extra diaper pins.

Where. Choose a warm, quiet spot for the bath. The kitchen table or bathroom vanity is usually a wise choice.

When. Bathe the baby at the same time each day—he'll soon learn to expect and enjoy his bath. Many mothers like to bathe the baby before the midmorning feeding, but you can pick whatever time suits you best. Don't, however, bathe him right after a feeding, as he needs a quiet time to follow his meals.

The sponge bath. Your doctor will probably recommend a sponge bath for your baby until the navel or circumcision is healed. For this, you can either hold the baby in your lap or lay him on a soft towel on the table where you have already placed the bath basket, clean clothing, and a small bowl of water around 95-100 degrees (this will feel comfortable to your elbow). Now you're set.

1. Clean outer nose and ears with cotton swabs.
2. Clean face with a cotton ball dipped in warm water.
3. Shampoo scalp three times a week and oil head daily. To rinse, hold baby's head and back over basin of water. Pat dry.
4. Remove shirt. Soap chest, arms, and hands, paying attention to folds and creases of skin. Rinse with warm water and pat dry. Turn baby over, soap back, buttocks. Rinse with warm water. Pat dry. Return baby to back and cover chest with towel.

The tub bath. Using a small plastic tub, with a towel placed on the bottom to prevent slipping, is one of the best ways to bathe an infant. I used to keep Heather's tub on a table about twenty-four inches high, right across from the toilet. This allowed me to sit down while bathing her, and provided a no-lift method of emptying the tub, as I simply tilted it into our big bathtub. Aside from putting baby into water, there's really not much difference between a sponge bath and a tub bath.

1. Shampoo hair first. To rinse, hold baby over tub in the crook of your arm. Dry hair before continuing bath.
2. Clean ears, nose, and face with cotton swabs and balls.
3. Undress baby and place him in the tub with one arm around him, supporting him at all times. Hold on to the outer arm for greater security.
4. Soap baby, rinse, and wrap immediately in towel. Pat dry. Powder, lotion, and dress. Continue with the plastic tub bath until baby is sitting up well. Then you might like to switch to the kitchen sink and gradually move on to the big bathtub as the baby shows readiness.

Some mothers grow to love bath time best of all, others never really like it—but all of us must learn to handle this job with cheerfulness and efficiency because the baby enjoys it so much. Today, bathing a baby may seem like a mountain; next year, however, you'll know it was scarcely a molehill.

DIAPERING

My baby brother Chris was born way back in the days of coonskin caps, bobby socks and, believe it or not, rosebud diapers. Now, the very sight of an eight-pound bruiser with floral print across his bottom is enough to catch a preschooler's interest. But what really fascinated me was that his diapers even smelled like roses.

"How could that be possible?" I had asked Mother. She pulled me aside and explained that a special sachet came with these diapers. She could even refresh the scent after washings. But after a few weeks Chris' diapers smelled like every other baby's, so the magic was gone. Still, there was something special about rosebud diapers, and I made up my mind, right then and there, that one day my own baby would wear them.

Twenty years and a pregnancy later, I began to hunt. It seemed, however, that the era of the rose-scented diaper was over. In its place was a highly sophisticated, if not downright complex, diapering industry which offered everything from comfort for Baby to convenience for Mom. There simply wasn't any other choice as far as I was concerned, but to purchase four dozen diapers—each dozen a different size, shape, and texture. The story of what became of these diapers is typical. Some of them became dust cloths, others found their way into new households, and a very small number proved so successful that I bought more. Oh, if only I'd known.

Diapering a baby is almost like combing your hair—everyone has her own style. And whether you decide to launder your own, make use of diaper service, or load up on disposables, you're in line for a lot of experimenting and a lot of mistakes before you find the one method that's for you. To get an idea of what's available, read the following facts, then take a quick survey through community shops to compare quality and price.

Laundering your own. If you're going to launder your own diapers, obviously you'll need to purchase some. Many people suggest three dozen for a starter. You might try this number until experience hints otherwise. Those using coin-operated washing machines, however, will probably enjoy the security of an extra dozen. You may be surprised at the wide choice of diapers awaiting you. There's gauze, cotton flannel, stretch cotton, and birds-eye for texture; square, rectangular, prefolded, and snap-ons for style; and newborn, large and extra large for size. A popular choice is gauze, because it dries quickly; rectangular because it can be folded in so many different ways; and large because it can be adjusted to fit any size baby.

You'll soon recognize the changing of a wiggly baby as an art within itself. In the beginning, you'll probably want to change your baby before and after each feeding. Simply fold the soiled portion of the diaper under, as you unpin. Place a waterproof pad under the baby to minimize mess. If he is only wet, there's no need to wash him, but after a bowel movement, you should wash the baby's bottom with cotton and water or one of the baby products designed for this purpose. Slip the clean diaper under the baby immediately, and bring it up between the legs. Pin on each side, back overlapping front, being careful to keep a finger between baby and diaper to avoid pin pricks. The older baby will need fewer changes, but continue to let odor and skin condition be your guide.

Six steps to diaper washing.

1. Purchase a diaper pail and a box of gentle soap powder. Following the directions on your soap carton, fill the pail with water and soap (usually a half cup of soap to a pail of water). Two tablespoons of chlorine bleach dissolved in hot water may also be added.

2. Scrape feces off, rinse diaper in toilet, and soak in pail.

3. When it's time to wash, pour off water and spin dry diapers.

4. Wash diapers in hot water.

5. Rinse twice.

6. Dry, but don't over-dry or iron diapers.

Now here's a trick for moms without automatic washers—skip the soaking. Flush out diaper in toilet, rinse in cold water, and place in a tightly sealed diaper pail. No, you won't have the prettiest diapers in the world, but you will save yourself from that thankless task of wringing out diapers by hand.

Diaper service. If you live in an apartment, you'll seriously want to consider diaper service. By the time you add up the cost of diapers, soap, and coin machines, there's little if any price difference between washing your own and having this service done for you. The company supplies and launders the diapers, saving you so much time and worry that even those parents with washing machines may consider it worthwhile.

About the only complaint against diaper service that I've ever heard is that they sometimes don't provide enough diapers in the early weeks of the baby's life. This can be worked out with the company, though, so don't discontinue for such a minor problem as this.

Disposables. Once again, we're up against a variety of styles and qualities. Disposables are wonderful for the mother on the go. And they're also popular with apartment moms on a generous budget. As a matter of fact, regardless of what you use during the day, disposable diapers can't be beaten for nighttime use, for they keep baby drier than cloth, and cut down on that ammonia smell that greets you each morning. Hints for using disposable diapers:

1. Buy good quality diapers. This will help to prevent diaper rash. The less expensive brands are seldom very absorbent, which simply means you'll be changing baby more often—making it all come out the same financially.

2. Avoid diaper pail odor—discard disposable diapers in a baggie with a twist tie.

3. When baby's wiggles cause you to damage stick-on tape tabs, secure diaper with ordinary diaper pin.

4. Save on plumbing expenses by emptying diaper in toilet and discarding in trash.

BEDDING

If at all possible, purchase a new crib for baby. Secondhand furniture is fine if you're buying from a trusted source, but that pretty garage sale buy could be painted with leftover paint that may contain lead. Then too, it may have slept as many as five successive babies, indicating that its best life is over. A friend of mine discovered that her secondhand crib had "had it," when nine-month-old Timmy literally shook the slats loose, and promptly fell out. At any rate, what's so bad about overspending on a bed with the first baby? This may be the last time you can justify frivolity on baby equipment.

Select a good firm mattress. If you own a washing machine, you might want to protect the mattress with a thick quilted cover—it will add comfort and warmth for baby as well. Apartment dwellers may find a plastic cover that zips on and off more practical. When baby soils the sheet, you have only to drop it in your diaper pail, and wipe the plastic cover clean.

A pillow can be added when baby is about a year old. Remember to remove it during bouts of sickness, though.

Bedtime is often unpleasant from the very beginning of baby's life. Perhaps it's because we expect too much. The young child is sometimes an erratic sleeper—going to bed as late as nine and waking for several hours of play at midnight. This can go on for some time, and you may find that you're ready for baby to adopt more civilized sleeping habits before he is. In that event, you'll have to teach him about sleeping. Try moving baby's bedtime up by fifteen minutes every week until you've reached a satisfactory time. Allow him to cry for a good twenty minutes, but any crying beyond this probably means you should wait awhile before pushing the issue.

While your baby is learning to sleep through the night, he may call out to you several times, and you can answer his cries with a short nursing, a glass of milk, or a pat on the back. Daddies sometimes have a magic touch with fretful sleepers.

Even after you've got bedtime all worked out, baby may revert to his old habits now and then. He may have had a bad dream, be teething, or be upset about something that happened during the day. Feel free to pick him up, rock him, or even carry him out to the center of family life.

Establishing a bedtime is important. First of all, you're teaching your child good health rules. But second, and just as important, you're providing a few hours of solitude for you and your husband. Those quiet hours between yours and baby's bedtime may be just what you and your husband need to get back in touch with each other after a day of being apart.

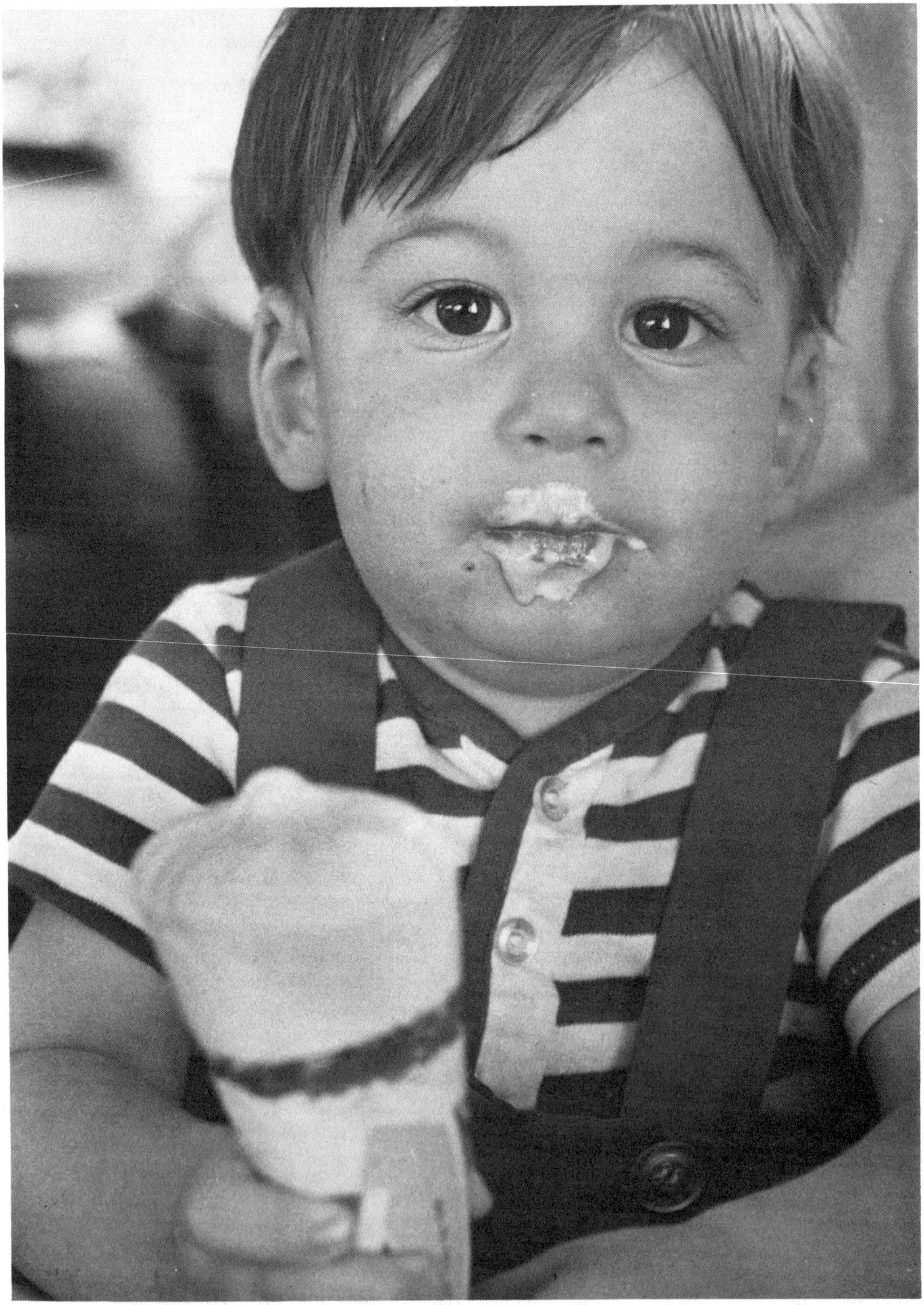

Feeding—food facts

In spite of all that's been said and done to enlighten mothers on the subject of infant feeding, some of us are still complaining of feeding problems. But it's the way we handle these so-called problems that can really be pathetic. Take Betty, for instance. She follows each bite of food that goes into three-month-old Karen's mouth with a pacifier. "Why are you doing that?" I asked.

"That, my friend, is how I get her to swallow her food," the triumphant mother replied.

I almost bit my tongue as I watched the baby gag on a cereal that looked and probably tasted much like shredded cardboard.

Then there's Susan. Feeling a tiny bit guilty, this woman apologized as she poured honey into her son's strained vegetables. "It's the only way I can get Tommy to eat," she explained.

But I wonder how this mother will feel when Tommy is ten years old and still leaning on sweeteners to disguise the taste of food?

If baby doesn't eat, Mother almost collapses from frustration. Why? Well, it *is* pretty awesome to be totally responsible for somebody else's nutritional well-being. I've often had visions, myself, of a health official knocking at the door, demanding custody of our "starving" child. And on my less imaginative days, I'm sure that any skinny legs or crooked teeth showing up in the next thirteen years will be blamed on none other than Mom. I suppose most of us are halfway willing to believe that babies will eat when they're hungry and that they shouldn't be pushed or forced, but there's always an auntie or a grandma around to ask, "Is he a good eater?" And that puts us right back where we started.

If you're undecided on how you'll feed your unborn baby, it might be worth noting that nursing mothers seldom have feeding problems. It's not that breastfed babies are such terrific eaters, it's just that these mothers don't worry about their babies' occasional refusal to eat. They know that the baby is getting his best nutrition from Mother. Then too, breastfed babies thrive on mother's milk for a good five months before graduating to mashed table foods, thus eliminating the intermediate step of bland-tasting commercial baby foods. On the other hand, bottle babies shouldn't become the victims of nagging, coaxing, or scolding just because they need the nutrients that solid foods offer at an earlier age. Eating is one of nature's pleasures and should be a pleasant experience even for the very young.

Think of those things that take away from the enjoyment of your own meals. Most of us don't like to be cold while eating. Remember how miserable you were the last time you ate in a restaurant that kept its thermostat too low? We don't like to be rushed while eating. Remember that last case of indigestion? We don't like to eat while people are arguing. Remember how that disagreement between your husband and his brother spoiled the Sunday roast? And we don't like to eat alone. Remember how you lost five pounds when your husband was away on business? But most of all, we don't like to eat tasteless, unattractively prepared food. Now think about your baby's last meal—how would you describe it?

The Bible mentions good food many times. Job throws light on the subject with his simple question,

Can that which is unsavoury be eaten without salt? or is there any taste in the white of an egg? (Job 6:6).

Today, mothers know two things about feeding babies that our foremothers could only wonder about. 1) Babies under the age of nine months don't need or care anything about table salt. They get salt naturally from their milk and from some of the foods they eat. 2) The tasteless white of an egg not only contains very little food value, it is a common cause of food allergies. Job's question wasn't meant to be cooking instructions, but I really don't think he would mind our borrowing it to serve as a guideline.

Any food which is either so tasteless that it requires seasoning, or of such little nutritional value that we can just as well do without it, isn't good baby food.

There are several ways to select your baby's food. First, read all that you can on the subject, then study food labels on the commercial foods, and last, perform your own tasting tests. Compare the flavor of commercial strained carrots and some freshly ground carrots that have been cooked in a small amount of water. Do the same with peas, beets, bananas, and so forth until you've got a fairly good idea of the areas in which you need to add your own touch.

But be fair to the baby food industry; some of their foods are adequately tasty, and contain very little, if any, sugar and salt. All of us, however, would do better to eat foods as close to their natural state as possible. This doesn't mean you're going to have to get into gourmet baby food cooking, it simply means that whenever possible, you'll feed the entire family fresh, unprocessed foods.

In order for baby to eat from the family table, you'll need a food mill for grinding his food to an easy-to-eat consistency and a weekly grocery list to help you plan interesting and nutritious meals. Babies are pleased with the simplest menus. You need only cook the food, grind it in your food mill, and then soften it with a little breast milk or formula. Following the doctor's instructions as to order of introduction, plan your baby's meals from the food list below. And don't forget your own imagination—baby will think those ideas best of all.

FRUIT

Bananas. An excellent first food, these can be mashed and softened with milk.

Apples. Can be cooked and run through a food mill for the young baby; peeled and cut into finger slices for the older baby.

Juices. Your doctor will advise you on the use of orange, pineapple, and prune juice. If you don't plan on making your own, do be sure to check the labels on juice bottles and stay away from sugar drinks.

Pears and peaches. The older baby will enjoy these fruits peeled and cut into finger slices.

Oranges and grapefruit. The older baby can also eat small segments of these fruits from which you've removed the seeds.

Other fruits. Some fruits are too tart by themselves for baby. This is one reason that sugar is often added to commercial baby food fruits. Be your own judge.

EGGS

Because egg white can cause allergy, wait for your doctor's signal before including this part of the egg. In the meantime, hard boil baby's egg so that the yolk can be easily separated from the white. Mashed with a little milk, egg yolk is often recommended by doctors as an early food.

VEGETABLES

Sweet potatoes. Another good early food, baked sweet potatoes can be mashed and softened with milk. White potato can be prepared in the same manner.

Carrots, squash, beets, asparagus, spinach, broccoli, green beans, and other easy-to-eat vegetables. Simply cook these vegetables in a small amount of water until tender, grind in your food mill, and soften with liquid. Older babies prefer their vegetables served as finger foods.

MEATS

Organ meats. These are good for the very young because they're so high in nutrition and of an easy-to-eat consistency. Beef and chicken liver, chicken gizzards, lamb or veal kidneys, brains, and sweetbreads can be braised or sauteed, run through your food mill, and softened with liquid.

Other meats. Fresh or frozen fish, chicken, ham, beef, veal, lamb, and turkey can also be braised or sauteed, ground in your food mill, and softened with liquid. Avoid roast or chops until baby is well on his way to eating "grown-up" food.

SNACKS

Your older baby will delight in carrot sticks, whole wheat toast, peanut butter on celery sticks, and puffed rice (one of the few sugar-free cereals). Ask your doctor about the use of cheese, yogurt, and butter, as the child that might be allergic to milk could also react to these products.

CHANGE OF SCENERY

As baby gets more active, he'll enjoy having his dinner served in the back of a clean plastic truck, eating from a real lunch box, and having an occasional breakfast in front of a children's television show.

There will no doubt be days on which nothing appeals to your baby's palate. This is when you'll cheerfully remove his food and try again later in the day. Perhaps he's teething, coming down with a cold, or just plain not in the mood. If baby is over nine months, he may be protesting for something a little tastier than highchair fare. Now you may want to add a dash of salt or a speck of catsup.

There's a lot that mealtime isn't. It's not an activity to erase boredom. It's not a chance for children to gain parental approval by cleaning their plates. It's not a contest between neighborhood friends to see who feeds her family the best. We eat to replenish our bodies of vital nutrients, and God has been kind enough to make this a pleasant necessity. Mealtime *is* an opportunity to enjoy savory food, and an opportunity to savor family love. Life savors—make sure that you, the Christian mother, serve both flavors.

Friends— Help! I'm lonely

Ever move to a strange city as a child? If you did, then you can remember the pain of being friendless in a neighborhood where everyone else was already "best friends." But if you've ever moved to a new community as a grown married woman, you've no doubt discovered that those old aches weren't just growing pains. Being a mother makes loneliness even more pronounced. Perhaps it's because getting out is more difficult now, or maybe it's because we don't have much in common with childless friends anymore. But whatever the reason, most of us would agree that motherhood is at times so demanding and frustrating that it seems impossible to go on without someone who understands.

Christian women thrive on friendship. You could even say it's part of our heritage, for the Bible is liberally spiced with stories of friendship. One of my favorites is of Mary, the mother of Jesus, and her cousin Elisabeth, the mother of John the Baptist. When Mary learned that she was to bear the Son of God, she packed her bags and went to visit her dear friend, Elisabeth, who was also pregnant. They had so much to share. Mary was, of course, an unmarried woman who had yet to face her fiancé and family. And while Elisabeth was having the dream of a lifetime come true, she was really extremely old to be having her first child.

And as if that weren't enough to worry about, her husband, Zacharias, hadn't been able to speak since the beginning of her pregnancy. So, bound with a thread of love found only among "best friends," these two women found comfort in each other's company for three whole months.

The beauty of Mary and Elisabeth's friendship is that it could have been yours or mine, for we too can remember times in our lives when our "best friend" was the only medicine that helped. But sometimes life finds us wishing for a friend instead of having one. Perhaps a young woman's new home removes her from a long-time circle of close friends, or a former career woman discovers that the role of mother is full of lonely hours. What happens then?

Well, some of us are like a neighbor I once had who was desperately trying to ignore her lack of friends. "I don't need any close friends," she grumbled to me over a cup of coffee. "My husband's my best friend."

You know, I still feel sorry for that woman— she's missing out on such a lot. By all means, our husbands are very special friends, and "best" in their own way. But if we're really honest, I think we'll have to admit that to expect a man to understand our most private thoughts is asking a bit much. Just as Mary and Elisabeth needed each other's companionship, we too, need the warmth of another woman's friendship.

Women often want to know how to go about making friends in a new community, or in the case of the career woman turned housewife, in the same community. It seems that no matter how many books we read on the subject and no matter how terrific these books sound, it's still very difficult to make new friends. "There's no one out there," is a common cry. But of course, this isn't true. There are many interesting people awaiting your friendship, and the adventure of finding them is likely to be one of life's richest experiences.

Walking is how I've met many of my neighbors. I never actually planned it that way; that's just how it always turned out. When you make it a habit to walk at the same time each day, you'll see the same people puttering about in their yards. Before you know it a friendly nod or hello will blossom into remarks about the weather, current news, and your child's latest antics. Suddenly, you've made a friend.

Then there are community-sponsored friendship clubs, church organizations, and even different modes of volunteer work such as hospital aid or community theater that offer excellent means of meeting new people. The YWCA has a special appeal to mothers because they do provide nursery facilities.

Make a list of your interests and decide which one you'd like to develop. The Sunday newspaper will have a variety of ideas to help you make up your mind as to how you can best use your time to make friends. Adult education classes, craft classes, bridge clubs, and tennis lessons are only a few ways to make new acquaintances with ease. Be sure, however, that you're truly interested in the chosen activity, for there's no value in joining a bowling league if you hate to bowl. Making friends should merely be thought of as a bonus from your hour of fun. Those of us who have moved a great deal will vouch that a relaxed, unhurried attitude on "friend-making" always seems to work best. In the meantime, you can gain a lot of satisfaction from an active correspondence with an old friend or pen pal.

Kahlil Gibran (*The Prophet*) tells us that a friend is the answer to our needs. But don't forget it works both ways. Once you've found that new friend, you'll feel like exploding with all the things you've been dying to share with someone. Just be careful about unloading confidential anxieties upon each other.

New friends handle positive exchanges best. Good news, recipes, craft ideas, funny stories, and books are a few things you might enjoy trading in the early days of a friendship. Then as your relationship grows, you'll want to strengthen it with acts of kindness. Offer your friend the use of your sewing machine, baby furniture, or camping equipment before she has to ask you. Compliment her on a clean house or a new hair style. Remember her birthday with a card, and make it a custom to exchange inexpensive Christmas gifts. Share a special Scripture verse with your friend, and tell her that you love her, for you do by this time.

Sorry, but that old saying, "To have a friend, you must first be a friend," is still true. Now it'll be your responsibility to take over when there's no one else to help your friend during a crisis. You'll also want to be sure to include her in your daily prayers, to be a source of encouragement, and to be available for fellowship when at all possible. Several things you'll dare not do are: offer your friend advice on her appearance, tell her how to manage her household, gossip about other friends, be pessimistic about her goals, and repeat unpleasant remarks that you've heard about her. But you wouldn't do anything like that, anyway, because

A friend loveth at all times
(Proverbs 17:17).

Games—
entertaining infants

A mother without magic is like a cook without a kitchen—not nearly as effective as she could be. Who else is going to teach restless junior how to turn handkerchiefs into dollies and church bulletins into airplanes? As baby grows older and wiser, your magic will have to become more mystical, but for a good year or two you can get by in the doctor's office or airport lounge with a few quiet-time games. Try to remember how your own mother entertained your younger brothers and sisters—the same tricks still work.

FINGER PUPPETS—a fist here and a finger there will turn the most ordinary hand into a delightful puppet. Use your imagination to come up with rabbits, deer, giraffes, and more. If you like, a face can be drawn on your hand with washable ink.

PAT-A-CAKE—one of the most popular and oldest of games, this little rhyme never fails to amuse a baby. Be sure to pat, roll, and mark the imaginary B with both your hands and Baby's, for these actions teach coordination as well as entertain.
> *Pat-a-cake*
> *Pat-a-cake*
> *Baker's man*
> *Bake me a cake as fast as you can.*
> *Pat it, and roll it, and mark it with a B,*
> *And put it in the oven for Baby and me.*

THE CHURCH—to make a church, interlock your fingers with the palms of your hands and fingertips facing you. Fold hands. Form the steeple with both index fingers; form the door with your thumbs. At the end of the verse, open the door and expose the interlocked fingers.
> *Here is the church*
> *And this is the steeple*
> *Open the door*
> *And see all the people.*

RIDE LITTLE HORSEY—cross your legs at the knees. Bounce baby on your ankle and at the end of the rhyme, gently slide him to the floor.
> *Ride little horsey*
> *Ride to town*
> *Better watch out or*
> *You'll fall down.*

THIS IS THE WAY—bounce baby on your lap, increasing tempo according to the rhyme.
> *This is the way the ladies ride.*
> *Trit-trot-trit-trot-trit-trot.*
> *This is the way the gentlemen ride.*
> *Trot-trot-trot-trot.*
> *And this is the way the farmer rides.*
> *Gallop-gallop-gallop-gallop.*

THREE LITTLE PIGS—could anyone forget this classic game? One group of mothers claimed that while they did remember the rhyme, some of the words were a bit hazy. Don't forget to tweak each toe as you chant.
> *This little piggy went to market.*
> *This little piggy stayed home.*
> *This little piggy had roast beef.*
> *This little piggy had none.*
> *This little piggy cried wee, wee, wee,*
> *All the way home.*

TWO LITTLE DICKY BIRDS—
> *Two little dicky birds (hold up two fingers)*
> *Sitting on a wall.*
> *One named Peter (flex one finger).*
> *The other named Paul (flex other finger).*
> *Fly away Peter (wave goodbye).*
> *Fly away Paul (wave goodbye).*
> *Come back Peter (beckon with hand).*
> *Come back Paul (beckon with hand).*

HOW BIG—ask the question, "How big is baby?" Then hold your arms high above your head. Before long, the baby will respond with the same gesture.

Grandmothers—grandma: that other woman in baby's life

It was our first day home. I sat stiffly erect in the recliner chair, awkwardly holding onto my most precious possession. Then little Heather cried, and the room was suddenly in turmoil—everyone wanting to help at once. It was my mother-in-law who won. I had ignored her outstretched arms for as long as possible.

"This is my baby," I wanted to shout. "Let me be the one to soothe and comfort her."

Besides, I was terribly afraid that while I might not be able to console Heather, my mother-in-law not only could, but would.

And just as I had suspected, Heather did indeed stop crying in her grandmother's experienced hands. My heart was broken. But I needn't have worried about my baby's apparent lack of loyalty, for as soon as those hunger pains began to gnaw at her tummy, Heather nestled closely against my warm body and vowed her love for me once again.

As for me? Well, I had learned a valuable lesson on my first day of "real" motherhood: grandmas and mommies don't have to compete for love, because there's plenty to go around; and yet, we often do.

It's sad when a child must grow up without a grandmother because of great distance separating the families, but it's much sadder when a child is denied the love of a grandmother because his mother has allowed friction between the two households to dominate. Sometimes this happens shortly after the birth of a first baby, when a well-meaning grandmother takes over the care of the newborn infant rather than just the house. Her advice and obvious adeptness often make the new mom feel completely inadequate, and secret or sometimes open resentment is born.

How wonderful it is when both women jump the generation gap and share their thoughts! Perhaps the grandmother could suddenly remember how she felt as a new mother and try to be more thoughtful, and maybe the new mother can discover that becoming a grandmother involves its own emotional trauma, and try to be more tolerant.

But unfortunately, this is one of those situations in which the new mother usually sits silently on the sideline, seething with an anger that never cools, and the tug-of-war begins.

Don't let this happen to you. Grandmothers can be a tremendous source of help to you, and will receive unimaginable joy from your child; but beyond that, grandmothers are special people who can add a dimension to your child's life that you yourself cannot give.

It seems that grandmothers have played a significant role in family life since the beginning of time. We can, in fact, find reference to them in the Bible. In one of Paul's letters to Timothy, he says:

I know how much you trust the Lord, just as your mother Eunice and your grandmother Lois do; and I feel sure you are still trusting him as much as ever
(2 Timothy 1:5, TLB).

It is believed that Timothy received a great deal of his religious instruction from his grandmother, Lois. Somehow, we can just picture him spending hours at his grandmother's feet, listening to her Bible stories, and who know, perhaps his mother felt pangs of jealousy at times. Nevertheless, like all wise mothers, Eunice must have encouraged these sessions, knowing how valuable they would be to her son and how meaningful they were to Lois.

Of course, it may be more difficult for some of us to step into the background while Grandma takes the limelight with our child, particularly if Grandma happens to be a mother-in-law. But she's part of your child's heritage. So, accept the bond of love between your baby and Grandma, recognize the value of the relationship, and go a step farther, by doing your part to nourish the alliance. You'll soon discover that it's no longer a duet, but a trio, because you're singing the love song too.

Here are eight points that deserve some attention if you're interested in giving your child the gift of a special grandmother.

1. Start from the beginning. Unless you and your husband are strongly opposed to the idea, invite your families to come over to your house for a brief "coming home from the hospital" party. If you don't really feel up to partying, excuse yourself to the bedroom, and leave the baby with his new relatives to croon over him to their hearts' content.

2. Whether Grandma is your mother, mother-in-law, or both, don't be stubborn. Enlist her help in those early weeks of your baby's life. Ask for specific favors such as preparing dinner, cleaning the bathroom, and changing the sheets. True gratitude will fill your heart, and at the same time, she'll feel as if she's on the inside of things. What could go wrong with such positive vibrations?

3. Acknowledge the fact that Grandma has indeed raised her family, so she really does know more about it than you. Of course, you'll not share all of her opinions on the proper way to care for a baby (every generation has its own child-care theories), but you'll listen courteously to her advice and remember it if some of your own ideas turn out to be "not so good." A pleasant statement such as, "Yes, that sounds like a good idea," isn't saying you're going to follow the suggestion.

4. Plan an outing now and then just to give Grandma an excuse for baby-sitting. Collect your little one in about two hours, so that both Grandma and the baby part with fond memories. Besides, as a new mother, you won't really be able to stay away from your baby much longer.

5. In the presence of Grandma, don't expect all of your rules to stick, but if Grandma is particularly bad about pushing the baby ahead to certain developmental stages that might prove dangerous, keep a few stumbling blocks in her way. Statements such as, "I really don't think our doctor would approve," or, "I'm so afraid he might choke on that," are difficult for any loving grandmother to ignore.

6. It's rare to find a child who doesn't think Grandma's cooking, knitting, sewing, and bedtime stories are better than Mom's. It's rarer still to find a child who isn't right about this. Try not to be jealous. Grandma's been doing all these things much longer than you have. Because she's probably got more time on her hands, and more patience than you, encourage your child to learn all that he can from his grandmother.

7. Grandmothers are famous for their old-fashioned remedies for colic, prickly heat, diaper rash, and bedwetting, and often their ideas are quite sound medically. Ask them for help whenever you need someone who really cares.

8. When the going gets rough, remember that tension between Mother and Grandmother is normal at first. But as you make a real effort to share your fears and joys of motherhood with this woman, you'll step on that common ground that's sure to make the two of you best friends, if you're not already.

Helps— mother to mother

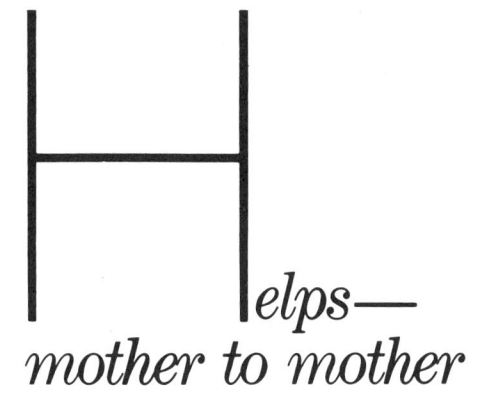

Listen to your father's advice and don't despise an old mother's experience (Proverbs 23:22, TLB).

Two heads really are better than one, so don't be surprised if some very good child-care hints come from interested friends and relatives. As the proverb says, please don't despise us when we thrust our suggestions upon you. Most of us learned these little secrets in exactly the same way you will—from other women:

When giving eyedrops or medicine by the spoon, wrap the baby's arms and legs in a towel. This frees your hands and cuts down on the kicking and squirming.

Tie the baby's favorite toy to his stroller with a string. Now he can play and *you* needn't worry about dropping rattles.

54 HELPS

Instead of investing in an expensive infant car seat, use a plastic infant seat intended for home use. Place baby and seat on the car's seat and secure safety belt through both. (As soon as the baby can sit with help, he needs to be in an approved car seat.)

Wipe runny noses with a warm washcloth. This helps keep that delicate skin from becoming irritated.

Try setting up your baby's bath on your ironing board. Not only can you move it to a warm area, but this is one table that can be adjusted to suit your height.

To keep you little one from slipping down in his highchair, place a rubber jar opener on the seat of the chair. This will provide just enough friction to keep your baby where you want him!

Broken glass in the kitchen? Make area safe by picking up glass splinters with a wet paper towel.

It's a good idea to take the phone off the hook during the baby's bath time. This will save you from frustrating attempts to reach the phone while keeping one hand on the baby. (If it's really important, the caller will know you're home and try again.)

When friends ask you what they can give you in the way of a baby gift, suggest a garment in one of the larger sizes.

Retain diaper pins' sharpness by sticking them into a cake of soap. (Some mothers make charming crocheted covers for the soap cake.)

Keep clean diapers unfolded in a large hamper. The type intended for the use of dirty clothes is excellent. Then, fold as you go.

Give the highchair an occasional shower bath. This is great for cleaning those hard-to-reach corners.

When the laundry turns up a stray sock, instead of searching for the mate, place the sock in a special box or basket. After a few washings you'll probably find that all of your lost socks can be matched.

As you hang nursery pictures, remember that your baby's eye-level is not the same as yours.

When serving a snack to adult company, don't forget the wee folk. A bowl of toasted whole wheat slices and puffed rice is a welcome treat to little ones.

Christmas with a baby in the house? Tie your tree to a nail that you've placed in the wall.

Laundry baskets make wonderful toy boxes that can be pushed under the crib for easy storage.

Put outgrown clothing away in clean, stain-free condition. You'll appreciate the effort when preparing for another baby.

To refresh the air in your baby's room, keep a solid air freshener on the dresser. Better remove this aid when the baby learns to climb, though.

Refurbish an old car seat with a cotton print upholstery job. Not only does your finished product look attractive, it will protect your baby's skin against a hot plastic seat.

Save the pretty paper that your baby's gifts came wrapped in. It can be made into a cherished collage for the nursery, or be used to line the dresser drawers.

If you don't fancy sharing your bathtub with your older baby's rubber duck, keep his bathtub toys all together in a fishnet shopping bag, and hang it over the shower nozzle.

On your baby's first birthday prepare a time capsule. In a shoebox, put an interesting variety of items that are of special significance to the year of his birth. A few ideas are: small New Testaments, souvenirs from vacations and fairs, newspaper clippings, postage stamps, coins, and photographs. Wrap the box in brown paper, tuck it in one of your drawers, and wait ten or twelve years before giving it to your child on another birthday.

Keep an extra tote bag loaded with goodies for entertaining the baby in difficult situations such as travel. Guaranteed to make any baby happy are: small boxes, plastic bottles without tops, wooden clothespins, sun glasses, hour glass, junk mail, a round cereal box, fancy ribbons, and a tiny address book.

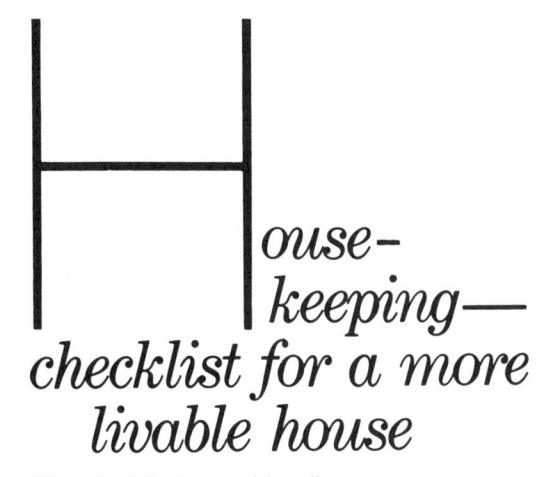

Housekeeping—
checklist for a more livable house

"If only I had a maid..."

Sound familiar? It probably does, if you're halfway human, because scarcely a new mother exists that doesn't think this thought at least once a day. Of course, there are those lucky women who can convince their husbands to take up post-partum housekeeping, but if you're not one of them, cheer up—there is a way to make your life easier. It's a matter of rearranging your household into a more workable order.

Grab a notebook and follow me through your house. We'll decide what Mom can do to make extra time for that catnap or those exercises.

THE BEDROOM

A comfortable, well-organized bedroom is a must for the new mother. Certainly, you'll clean out drawers and closets before the baby arrives, but don't forget to put away dust collectors—simplicity will help keep things neater. Now check your furniture. Although you shouldn't go to the extreme of squeezing a new bedroom suite into the budget, it's entirely possible that an inexpensive buy from a secondhand store might make a big difference in your comfort. Some things to consider are:

1. The bed—king, queen, or twin, any size bed will feel good to the tired mother—she just wants to be in it. But do give your mattress a fair evaluation. After wrestling with a new baby all day, both husband and wife need as restful a night as possible, and nothing is worse than a lumpy mattress. Not the time to make a major purchase? Perhaps new ticking would be the answer. Whatever you should decide about the mattress, you'll still want a mattress pad, at least two sets of sheets, a pretty quilt or blanket, and a backrest of some kind. Mothers who spend a lot of time in bed with the baby, and nursing mothers usually do, will find that bedrails give added peace of mind.

2. The rocker—most rockers are chosen with just about as much care as a house. But even so, we sometimes discover too late, that those beautiful ornate spindles are "backbreakers." You'll spend enough time in this piece of furniture to make the investment of cushions worthwhile. And if the budget allows, it's nice to have a rocker in both the nursery and your bedroom.

3. Small items—it's a special luxury to have a television set in your bedroom, but even a radio will provide a lot of entertainment. Don't forget a wastepaper basket beside your bed and a nightlight for those two o'clock feedings. Some mothers like to keep a large cardboard box in one corner of the room so that when bric-a-brac becomes overwhelming, everything can be swept quickly into the box and out of sight. (You can do the sorting later when there's more time.)

THE KITCHEN

Because you're the mother and responsible for your family's nutritional welfare, the state of your kitchen during these postpartum days is of prime importance. If there's any rearranging of the cabinets to be done, enlist the help of your husband. It's wise to keep things that you use most often on the shelves that are easiest to reach, even if it does mean you'll be keeping party dishes under the sink and soap powder on your coffee mug shelf. A lot of clutter can be eliminated by clearing off an entire shelf just for baby's formula equipment, and even if you're nursing, you'll want to reserve a place for the food mill and such. If you simply can't spare the space, place baby's equipment in a plastic utility tray and keep it in a handy spot on the counter. Now while you've got Hubby's help, go ahead and move all poisons such as furniture polish and toilet bowl cleaner to an out-of-the-reach area, and you've just saved yourself the trouble of doing this job in a few months with a little one underfoot.

Keep kitchen gadgets orderly and easy to find with drawer dividers, hang pots and pans on a pegboard (to avoid excessive stooping), and make a list informing helpful relatives and your husband of the whereabouts of common utensils. At last, you're ready to stock the pantry.

In addition to having plenty of staples on hand, and as much meat and vegetables as your freezer will hold, you'll want a generous supply of nourishing snacks. A few items you'll find nice to have on hand are: cheese spread, tuna, canned luncheon meat, sardines, salmon, ravioli, canned soup, tamales, instant pudding, fruit juice, spaghetti sauce with meat balls, pasta, dried fruit, instant breakfast drinks, and breakfast bars and squares. Undoubtedly these foods are notoriously "processed," but if you really don't feel like cooking, they do offer more food value than some of the other options. And it won't be long before you're back in the kitchen at full swing, anyway. When you do start cooking, don't forget the marvelous convenience of cooking in aluminum foil and eating off paper plates.

HOUSEKEEPING 57

LIVING-DINING AREA

With visitors coming in and out, your living-dining area will probably suffer accordingly. To help keep things as tidy as possible, put away all decorative ornaments. Collect stray odds and ends that accumulate during the day in a large straw basket, and throw an attractive cover over your sofa to protect it from spills and little visitors' feet. In an out-of-the-way corner, set up a TV tray to hold diapers and baby supplies. It might not look chic, but it'll more than pay off in steps saved. Most mothers find that a small bed or cradle kept in this part of the house is a must. But again, the idea is more important than the equipment. Your baby will be perfectly comfortable nestled in blankets on a pallet of quilts.

THE BATHROOM

When it comes to the family bathroom, you deserve cooperation, so be firm. Insist that each family member hang his bath towel up to dry after use. If your bathroom doesn't have a dirty clothes hamper, improvise with an empty laundry basket. Give the sink a quick weekly scrub, use a hard soap that leaves little bathrub ring, keep blue cleanser in the toilet's water box, place several throw rugs on the floor to catch water and dust—and bathroom chores are cut in half.

THE NURSERY

The baby's room will be the least of your housecleaning problems. In fact, for a good nine months, it might be the only room you can call truly clean. No doubt, you've spent a lot of thought on baby's furniture. You will, however, want to be sure that everything is in a workable arrangement. Place a table beside the baby's bed. An inexpensive metal appliance cart is ideal as it has three shelves on which you can place various supplies. The bottom shelf works well for blankets, sheets, and lap pads, the middle shelf is a handy reachable height for diapers, and the top shelf is obviously where you'll want to keep the baby's toilet articles. Magazine articles and books on child care will tell you just what items are necessary for the maintenance of a newborn, but don't overlook your own imagination. Professionally made lists rarely include things like soft toilet tissue and radios. To avoid clutter, you might want to cover a box in bright adhesive paper and keep your ensemble neatly within.

You may not have a chest for baby just yet, but you'll want your substitute close by. A playpen makes a lovely temporary garment holder, or you can spread a clean bath towel on the floor near the crib and stack on it the gowns and T-shirts you'll be using during the early weeks.

OTHER ROOMS

When there are older children in the family, you may be at a loss as to what to do about their rooms. Ignore them. A new family member forces adjustment on everyone, even teenagers, and this is no time for daily room inspections. If you're going to ask your family for help during those early weeks, get it where it counts. Let your husband and any capable children aid you in the vacuuming, dusting, and mopping of the main living areas. But don't stir up discontent by asking for too much help. Even though you love your house and take pride in keeping it clean, when all is said and done, without harmony within, your house can never be a home.

It is better to dwell in a corner of the housetop, than with a brawling woman in a wide house (Proverbs 21:9).

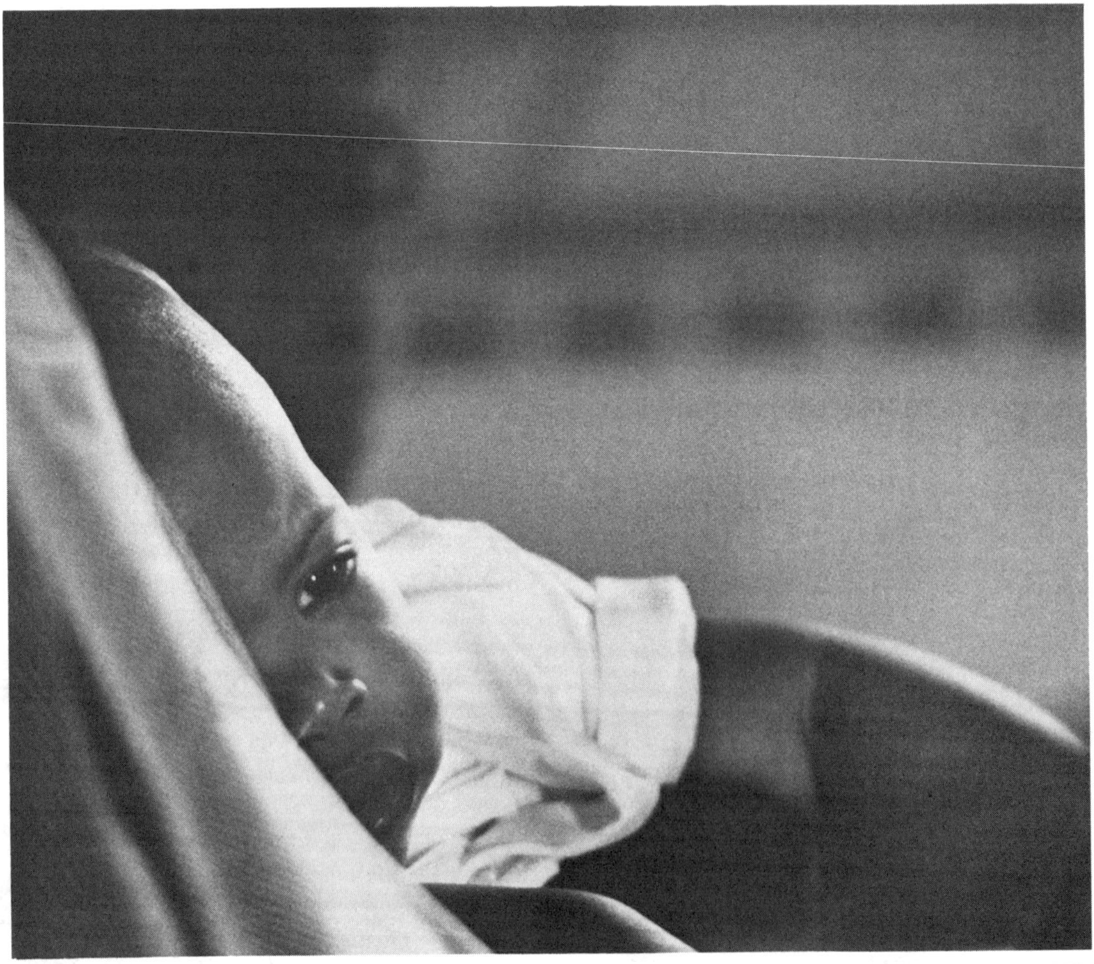

Illness— temperature's rising

No one wants to anticipate illness. It's kind of like waiting for the sun to burn out—too dreadful to even think about, much less prepare for. But be forewarned, your baby will get sick now and then. Maybe you'll glide through all the way up to teething, then suddenly the odds for sickness are so great you can scarcely plan a vacation or look forward to an evening out. You feel disappointed, a little bit afraid, and even a trifle embarrassed at the baby's unpredictable health. No wonder that simply "coping" becomes your major goal from day to day.

If there's any time that being a Christian is a bonus, this is it. For when it comes to a sick baby, there is no person on earth and no book in print that can give us the same peace of mind as God. What a shame that God is more often than not our last resort—the one we go to when modern medicine won't make any promises. And the main thing wrong with this sort of thinking is that we've got it all backward. A more sensible approach to illness is to get in touch with God first, our doctor second, and those baby books last. Here's how it works.

PRAYER

Baby is sick. You know it for a fact because of a different cry, a rise in temperature, a rash, or some other unusual symptom. You start to panic, to rush for the thermometer and the telephone all at once, but a red light flashes in your mind and you stop—you carry the baby to a quiet spot and begin your prayers.

There are many different opinions on praying the healing prayer, and if you have a favorite and workable method, stick to it. I find the prayer of relinquishment most effective. You turn your loved one and his illness over to God. It's too much for you to handle, so you don't. This means no worry and no dread on your part; it's now in the hands of God.

For some people prayer comes naturally and effortlessly even in times of stress, but if you haven't found this to be true, you can train yourself to make it so from now on. A friend of mine keeps an empty medicine bottle labeled "prayer" in her medicine chest so that when she rushes for a remedy, prayer slows her down. Other Christian mothers like to anoint a sick one with kitchen oil as they pray. This provides a point of contact, and seems to help make the communication more intense.

CALLING THE DOCTOR

When you call the doctor, you should have the following information written down on a piece of paper.
1. Baby's symptoms and how long he has had them.
2. Baby's temperature.
3. The names and amounts of any medicine you might have given on your own.

If you must leave your phone number with the doctor's answering service, be sure to stay at that particular location until the doctor has returned your call.

READING BABY BOOKS

After I've received the doctor's diagnosis, I drag out my baby books and read up on the problem. This gives me a better understanding of the diagnosis and reinforces confidence in the physician's decision. Sometimes the doctor is even wrong. In this case, my baby books give me suggestions to offer him. If you should choose to follow this pattern, however, be careful that you never refer your doctor to your books.

PRACTICAL HINTS
ON CARING FOR YOUR SICK BABY

Temperature. Always take your baby's temperature rectally, rather than under the arm. This procedure is the more accurate of the two and is usually the physician's choice.
A rectal thermometer has a shorter bulb than an oral one, but in a pinch, it hardly matters which one you use. You will, of course, want to put a little petroleum jelly on the bulb so that it will slip into place without irritating baby's skin. A small baby can be placed on his back or stomach while you take his temperature, but the wiggler is easier to handle on his stomach.

Let the older baby play with some usually forbidden item such as an alarm clock or telephone and hold the thermometer in place for three to five minutes, depending on when the mercury stops climbing. Read the thermometer, remembering that a normal rectal reading is one degree higher at 99.6. But if you're calling the doctor, he will want the temperature exactly as it reads, so don't try to transpose it into an oral equivalent. Wipe the thermometer clean with a tissue and wash it with soap and cold water.

When fever is high. A baby's temperature can shoot sky high at a moment's notice. You'll want to avoid temperatures around 105 degrees and higher, as convulsions may result and scare the life out of *you*. Make sure that you know the proper dosage of aspirin and aspirin substitute. When fever is high, most doctors will allow you to give both drugs at alternating two-hour intervals. A sponge bath of alcohol and water is also helpful for lowering baby's temperature. Fever is a sign that something is not quite right, be sure to contact your doctor.

Dressing the sick baby. Keep baby dressed in soft, comfortable clothing for the duration of his illness; no scratchy lace or tight armholes, please. If diarrhea is a problem, you may want to dress baby in a gown rather than a knitted suit with feet in it. Do give a daily bath and change soiled garments promptly. Some mothers keep one special pair of pajamas to be worn to the doctor's office only, and you might be surprised at the VIP service these mothers receive at the clinic.

The sick baby's room. A nursery turned infirmary should be warm and free of drafts. Buy or make a mobile to hang over the crib, and change linens frequently. Protect objects such as pillows and toys from becoming accidentally soiled by removing them from the bed. Respect baby's need for quiet and prohibit the use of television and radio in his room. There may be occasions when you'll make him a bed in the living room, or perhaps tuck him in bed beside you, but allow baby to rest in his own crib for as long as he wants.

Feeding the sick baby. Sick babies are not really going to eat much, but whether your baby is completely breastfed or well into solids, ask your doctor to be specific about his diet. Don't be tempted to coax baby's appetite; he'll eat when he's ready. In the meantime, it might be helpful to remember that during infections and fever, proteins are used up quickly, so smaller, more frequent feedings are advised—usually a liquid, semiliquid, or soft diet.

> *Clear liquid diet*—clear soup such as chicken broth, 7-UP.
>
> *Liquid diet*—cream soups, plain ice cream, fruit juices, meat broths.
>
> *Soft diet*—baked potato, cream cheese and crackers, gelatin, angel food cake.

When it comes to diarrhea, baby's diet will depend upon the cause. You'll probably be told to begin with liquids and gradually add solids. The intestine is irritated and needs the rest, so too little food is better than too much.

Handling yourself. Now's the time when you're not sure who feels worse—you or the baby. You've gone hours without sleep, food upsets your stomach, and your patience has gone to the wind. Take time out on your next trip to the bathroom to pray once again your prayer of relinquishment. Sure, you turned that baby over to God, but the devil is right there beside you trying his best to destroy your faith.

Call a friend or relative (preferably a grandmother) to take over a few hours of rocking. You might find this time useful for catching a quick nap, or you may want to spend nervous energy by doing some knitting or simple needlework. Keep your house as orderly as possible to avoid that "sick house" feeling, and don't neglect your daily exercise. A round of calisthenics or a walk down the block will do wonders for recharging your energy.

When a friend called me up and said, "Praise the Lord, Lisa's cold is gone," I knew just what she meant. I'll bet by this time, you do too.

And the prayer of faith shall save the sick . . . (James 5:15a).

Ingenuity—the gift of love

It is more blessed to give than to receive (Acts 20:35).

But wait a minute—is it always? I mean, what happens when the obligation to give begins to outweigh the fun of it all? Certainly we *can't* overlook the celebrations of friends, business partners, and special clients. And surely we don't *want* to overlook people in need. But even so, the birth of a baby leaves our own finances somewhat depleted. What to do?

A lot of us are falling back on that age-old commodity—ingenuity. And for good reason, too. It's like money in your pocket. It'll buy anything from a backyard circus to a collection of handsome paper dolls, costs virtually nothing, and is wrapped unabashedly in love. You couldn't do better than that at the most exclusive shop in town.

Creative gifts add a sparkle to any occasion. I remember attending a baby shower one time when a young woman presented the mother-to-be with a pretty bottle of brewers yeast. She labeled the bottle "energy" and attached directions for mixing with orange juice. Not only was the expectant mother genuinely pleased, but the novelty of this inexpensive gift seemed to rejuvenate the party with fresh enthusiasm.

But a word of caution. Such giving is incurable once you've really caught the bug. You'll find yourself writing ideas down on menu planners, book marks, even church bulletins. Perhaps a small box in your closet will soon store things you once thoughtlessly discarded—pretty ribbons, unusual boxes, interesting bottles. For you'll have discovered that, stripped of its financial burden, giving is indeed more pleasurable than receiving.

Here are a few of my favorite gift ideas. Don't forget to prop baby up where he can watch you assemble gifts—generosity is a learned habit.

For that new mom:

1. Something special from your own baby's layette will make a nice addition to the little one's wardrobe. Just make sure that the garment is free of stains and has all its snaps and buttons intact.

2. Baby-sitting certificates can be a real boon to the new mom. Type or print your offer on a decorated note card and slip it in an envelope.

3. A box of assorted tea blends will come in handy during those last weeks of waiting, as well as during the first weeks of coping.

4. Check with your bookstore for new releases on nursing and child care.

5. Give a box of disposable diapers—no one will put you down for this gesture.

6. For the avid reader, collect magazine fiction depicting new mothers, tie the collection with a red ribbon, and label "for hospital reading."

7. Try your hand at an inexpensive wall-hanging. Decopage, needlepoint, macrame, and embroidery can become your baby shower trademark.

8. Make an attractive "Do Not Disturb" sign for Mom to hang on her front door during baby's nap.

9. Decorate three plastic butter dishes with contact paper, fill respectively with cotton balls, cotton swabs, and a bar of delicate soap.

10. If there are other children in the family, consider giving them a gift. Board games,

INGENUITY

coloring books, or craft kits can occupy youngsters while Mom's in the hospital.

For a recuperating friend:

1. Sometimes people who might not feel up to reading take great pleasure in a catalog. Round up a seed catalog for the gardener, a stitchery catalog for the needlework fan.
2. An interesting stack of travel brochures can often cure sick room doldrums.
3. How about gathering up all those loose recipes stuck into your cookbook and sharing them with an enthusiastic cook?
4. Make a scrapbook of animal cartoons—sure to make anyone smile.
5. If there's a photographer in the family, lend a box of scenic slides and a slide viewer.

For someone special of any age:

1. Give a homemade bath relaxer made of soda and salt.
2. Collect coupons and slip inside a friendship card.
3. Make a seed sack out of a small cotton square. Simply sew up three sides of the square, turn, fill with seeds, and tie with a ribbon or rickrack.
4. Make your own craft kits. Sewing kits, decoupage kits, and the like can be assembled inexpensively by you.
5. Delight a youngster or a talented adult with a generous supply of cornstarch clay. Blend 2 cups soda and 1 cup cornstarch. Add 1¼ cup cold water. Mix until smooth. Stirring constantly, boil 1 minute or until the consistency of mashed potatoes. Spoon onto plate, cover with damp towel, and cool. Knead lightly. Store in airtight container until ready to use.
6. A decorated cardboard file holder will house coupons, letters, and much more.
7. Wrap a small present in gobs and gobs of yarn until you've formed a ball. The suspense of unwrapping is half the gift.
8. Surprise a friend with an imported candy bar.

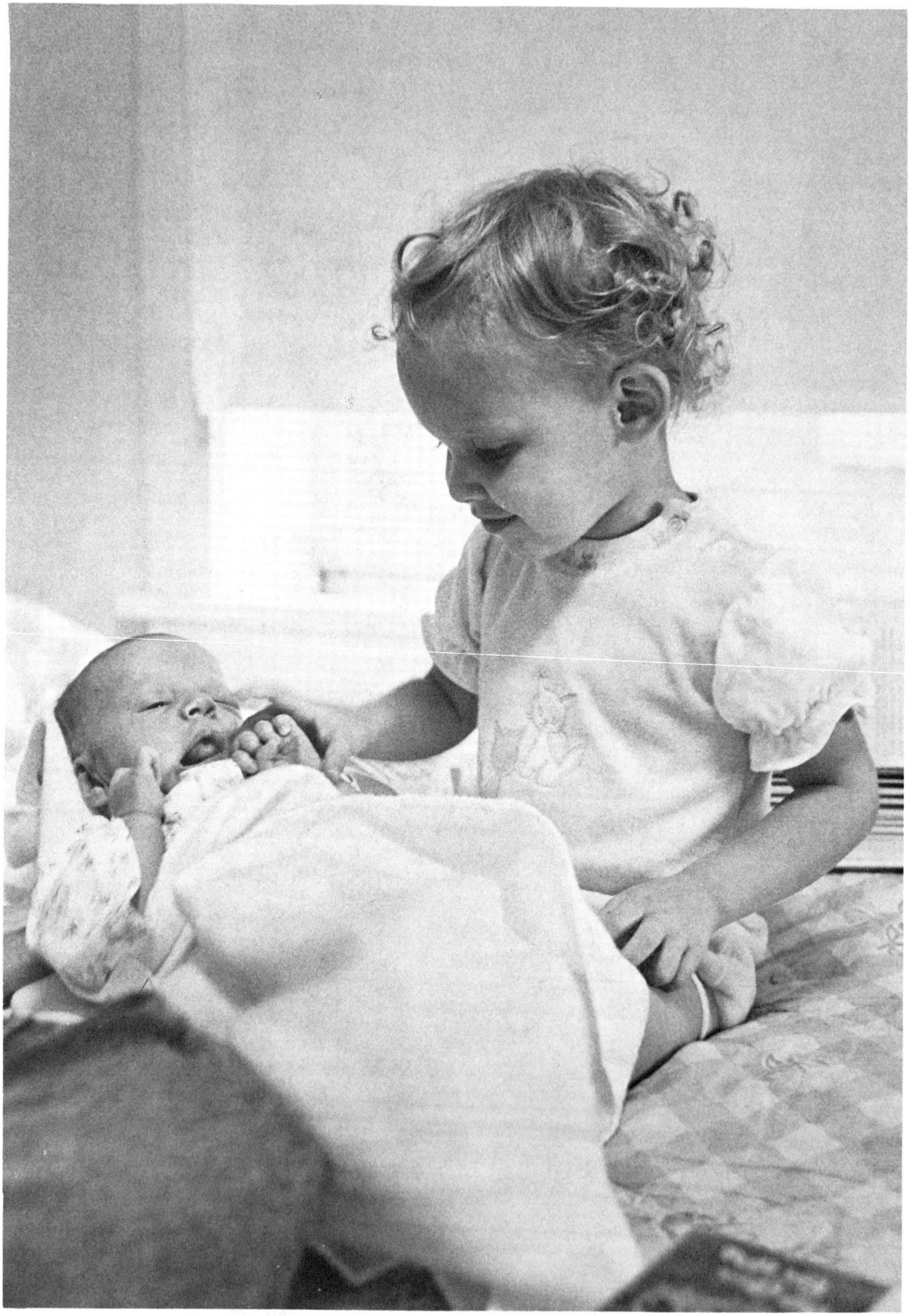

Jealousy—building on

When Mother presented our already "completed" family with a postscript baby, everyone looked cautiously toward six-year-old Noel for telltale signs of jealousy. Imagine their confusion when it was not Noel, but the teenagers of the family who began to throw tantrums of insecurity. I'll not attempt to say why or how this happened—I don't know. I'm merely pointing out that one never knows which family member will undergo the most emotional stress upon the arrival of a new baby.

Jealousy is one of those unpredictable evils, and even if this is your first baby, you can expect someone to succumb to it. For when a new family member arrives on the scene, other children sometimes feel unloved, husbands sometimes feel neglected, and you, yourself, will probably admit to feelings of resentment now and then.

No one can help you avoid a jealousy crisis. It may, in fact, be a necessary step in family growth. But if you will recognize the problem and actually cater to it, things should go a lot smoother. Think of your pregnancy as "building on." If you were adding a new room to your house, you certainly wouldn't let the rest of your home fall into shambles. The finished product is to be a larger house, not just another room. It's the same with a baby. You're widening and strengthening your family, not just creating one child. So take care of your family and keep it united with love and thoughtfulness.

You can make a good start by considering each family member right from the beginning. Let your children know of your pregnancy before you've told the next-door neighbor and your friends across town. Explain to them that you don't feel very well (if such is the case), but that you're happy to be having another child.

Next comes the matter of space. Where's baby going to fit? You may think that only adults worry about such details, but don't kid yourself. If big brother or sister stands a chance of losing privacy, he or she will be frantic with concern. Go ahead and solve this problem early in your pregnancy, for the sooner it's settled the happier everyone will be. When an older child must share his room with either the baby or another, much younger child, you owe him a tiny nook of privacy. And no, lack of money is not an excuse.

If nothing else, make your own room divider by stretching fabric across a wooden frame and stapling it in place. When sharing even extends over to the chest of drawers, don't expect a child to make do with half the space he once had. A small trunk pushed under or placed at the foot of his bed will accommodate the overflow.

Since we know that a baby will cause a change in routine, why add this adjustment to postpartum recovery? Begin initiating the family to change several months in advance of baby's arrival. I once knew a little girl who enjoyed jumping into bed with her pregnant Mom as soon as Daddy left for work. The two of them often slept the morning away like this until the wise mother realized it could not continue after the baby arrived. So she used the last month of her pregnancy to break her daughter of the habit by insisting that everyone be up and dressed for an early breakfast. The new arrangement worked well and neither mom nor daughter resented the baby for taking away their special nap time, for they had already adjusted.

Change of routine doesn't always involve young children, though. What about the childless couple who is used to going on business trips together, or the teenager who'll soon be expected to help out with a few household chores? They too need to ease into the situation.

As you prepare for the baby, include the other family members. While you're sewing baby clothes, take time out to run up a supply of easy-care garments for the older children, and check your hubby's wardrobe for needed purchases.

You might also consider spending odd moments on a jolly jar. This is a decorated quart jar that you will fill to the brim with activity suggestions. Everything from circus day to a Chinese parade should be written on a small piece of paper and dropped into the jar. Then when your children begin to roam the house with restless boredom, you've got a ready-made solution on your hands.

Another idea is to stock up on quiet time toys. Remember, however, these are to be stored until after baby arrives. Have long-term plans because you really won't feel up to pampering your family for awhile. Who knows, a size four romper, cleverly tucked away in your dresser drawer, may be just what your three-year-old needs to boost his morale six months from now.

Your hospital stay may be particularly trying for the rest of the family. Perhaps you'll want to give each family member a gift from the new baby. (My husband and I exchanged gifts when our daughter was born as a symbol of celebration.) If visiting hours exclude children, you might even fill your suitcase with an assortment of inexpensive toys to send home with Daddy each evening. And of course a picture of baby is everyone's right, even though your toddler is likely to chew it. You can keep in touch each day via the telephone, and if you're really industrious, you can arrange for a set of ready-made letters to arrive via "stork express."

Once you've come home, allow the other children to hold the baby, and yes, breathe in his face. (There's no use in fighting this.) You may be surprised when your four-year-old soils his underpants, and a bit shocked when your two-year-old decides that he too will be breastfed, but take heart, these problems won't last long. Experienced mothers have reported great success with the following ideas.

1. Brag often about what wonderful help your older children are.
2. Arrange for relatives or Daddy to telephone just to speak to the jealous child.
3. Plan father and child outings.
4. Leave the baby with Dad and take your older children shopping.
5. Keep inexpensive surprises hidden in your cabinets. These serve as special boosters.

This may all sound easy enough, but what if Mama or Papa is the troubled one in your household? Stella Chess, physician and writer, tells us that for a parent to be jealous of his new baby is also quite normal and very common. We give up a little more freedom and a little more youth for each child that we have. And when there's never any time to take care of your own needs, it's easy to begin resenting baby. This problem is probably more common among women than men. We're the ones that have sagging bellies, unattractive stretch marks, and circles under our eyes. And we're the ones that no longer have time for entertaining or strength for going out.

Dear me, the list of complaints could go on and on. Our husbands, however, are quick to strike back with the fact that we're always too tired for lovemaking, never have time to listen, and seem to have lost all understanding of the working person's life.

Don't hide these feelings. Admit to Hubby that you're jealous when he leaves for work all clean and freshly shaven. (He'll probably shock you into your senses by giving you the go-ahead to return to work.) Ask for help when you need it, but be specific. A generalized plea for help usually only results in an argument, while a direct request brings quick action. Last of all, share your worries so that the two of you can extinguish them together. Does your figure bother you? Perhaps Hubby should encourage you by exercising alongside of you. Is it low self-esteem that's getting you down? Maybe your husband can come up with a worthwhile community project for you to become involved in.

When it comes to a jealous husband, take a look at yourself first. If you're happy, and feeling well, you'll find it easy to be attentive and loving to Hubby. But if things haven't begun to work themselves out by the baby's ninth month, you may want to consider confiding in a physician. He can turn you in the right direction for help. Don't judge your progress by another person's, though. You may need just a little more time.

Ignore jealousy? Never. As proof of the ultimate harm it can do to a family, reread the story of Esau and Jacob (Genesis 27:1-41). An old-fashioned remedy for handling the "bug" is:

1 oz. of recognition
2 lbs. of attention
Sprinkle with love and kiss goodbye.
Sound a bit phony? Better take another look, I've never known this recipe to fail.

Joy—
joys of a woman

What is joy? One woman sees it, another woman smells it, and another woman swears it can only be heard. Listen as Christian women from across the nation share their special joys with you; the variety is pure fun in itself. Be sure to jot down all letters in bold-faced print—they spell out a secret message.

I am most happy when...

Listening to Beethoven and kneading bread. *C. M., Seattle, Washington*

Remembering the words to an **o**ld love song. *N. Y., Lincoln Nebraska*

Baking a German **c**hocolate cake. *M. G., Dallas, Texas*

Holding a newborn kitten. *K. T., Kansas City, Kansas*

Experimenting with a new craft idea. *S. H., Duluth, Minnesota*

Buying a lens for my camera. *L. J., Des Moines, Iowa*

Day**d**reaming at the kitchen sink. *I. O., Birmingham, Alabama*

Reaching the top of a mountain. *N. R., Portland, Oregon*

Eating a tray of pastri**e**s. *E. C., Tulsa, Oklahoma*

Nursing my baby. *P. N., Rochester, New York*

Picking **a** bouquet of fresh flowers. *B. I., Vicksburg, Mississippi*

Running a mile in the early morning. *K. A., Oakland, California*

Reading a book with a happy **e**nding. *J. M., Chicago, Illinois*

Relaxing in **a** tub of hot water. *S. R., Boise, Idaho*

Taking a **n**oon siesta. *F. E., Santa Ana, California*

Helping my husband with the lawn. *S. J., Louisville, Kentucky*

Eating my way through a banana split. *D. P., Youngstown, Ohio*

Riding my ten-speed in the country. *E. J., Shreveport, Louisiana*

Potting new ivy plants. *O. R., Charlotte, North Carolina*

Talking on the telephone to friends. *D. O., Milwaukee, Wisconsin*

Wearing a new dress. *P. K., Tampa, Florida*

Giving a gift to a loved one. *C. E., Little River, Arkansas*

Feeling healthy and energetic. *S. M., Memphis, Tennessee*

Riding on a merry-go-round. *L. G., Salem, Oregon*

Finding a field of wild flowers. *B. C., Scranton, Pennsylvania*

Thinking private thoughts. *D. C., Tucson, Arizona*

Spending the afternoon with just my husband. *E. L., Winston Salem, North Carolina*

Digging my hands into fresh-smelling earth. *L. R., Syracuse, New York*

Feeling that first labor pain. *R. W., Denver, Colorado*

Living near the ocean. *B. B., Boston, Massachusetts*

Raking golden leaves. *L. T., Grand Rapids, Michigan*

Discovering a new landscape to paint. *M. E., Lubbock, Texas*

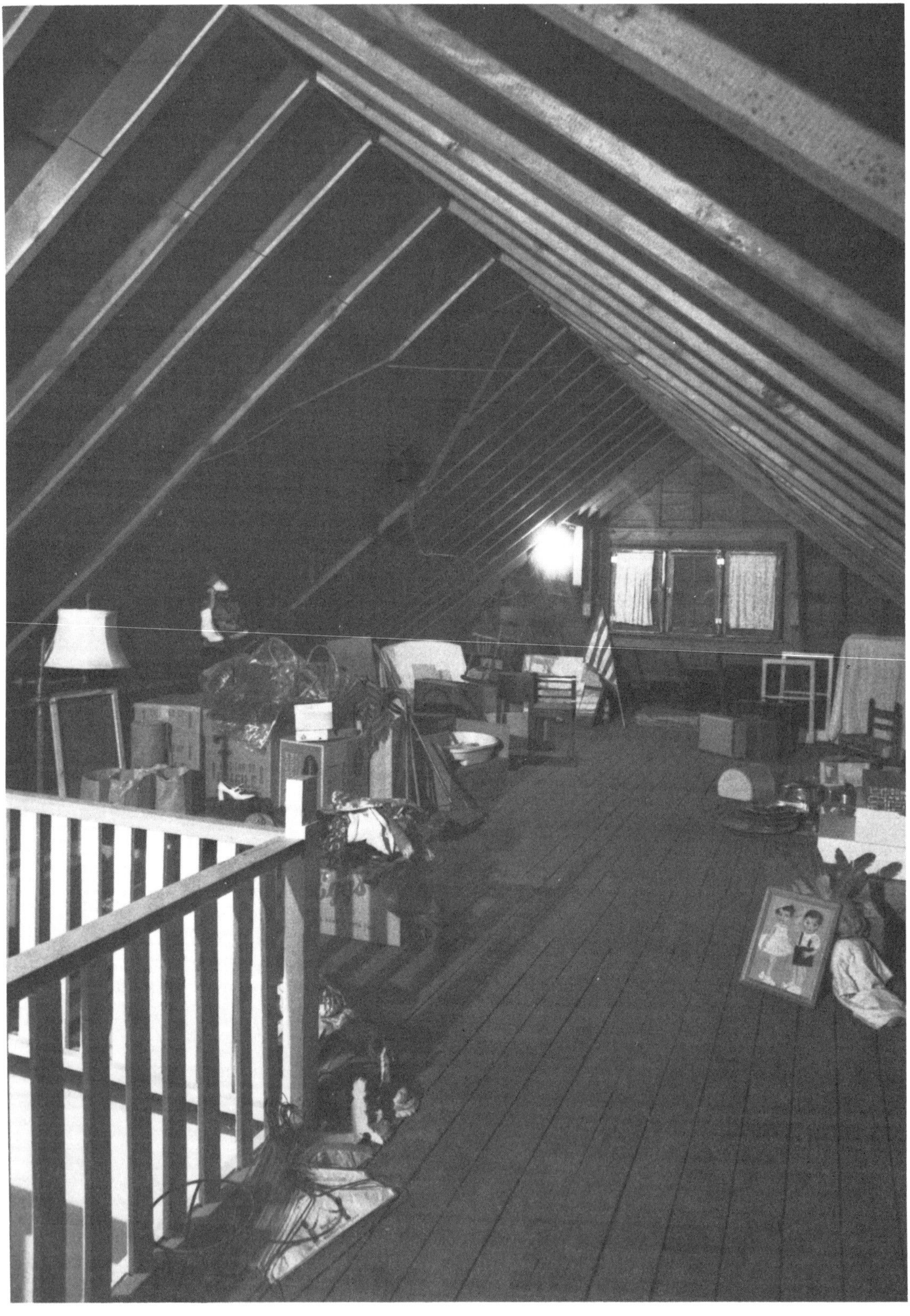

Keepsakes— making your own memory book

From my journal:
> *... Heather is thirteen months old today. Already, that first birthday, which once seemed so far in the future, is a part of the past. Where did time go? And why do I feel such a sense of loss? But of course, I know. For every day, my daughter becomes less of a baby and more of a child....*

There is probably no first-time mother who is really prepared for the briefness of infancy. If we could only push an instant replay button, most of us would be happy to relive every stage of baby's development. But since we can't go back into the past, our best alternative is to enjoy the present—every minute of it. It's the happy, relaxed life style of "now" that'll fill your heart with memories. And someday, just remembering will seem important.

The Bible tells us that Mary cherished certain memories of Jesus.

> ... *and his mother stored away all these things in her heart* (Luke 2:51b, TLB).

Today there are many ways to make remembering an easier job: photographs, tape recorders, journals, and scrapbooks, to name just a few. I like the idea of a scrapbook because it is inexpensive and demands little of Mom's time. You may have been lucky enough to receive one of the elaborate memory books that people so often give as shower gifts. If not, the following directions will tell you how to create a real treasure in little or no time.

Materials needed:
- A loose-leaf scrapbook held together with twine—available at most variety stores.
- About 1 yard of fabric. Choose from silks, dotted swiss, organza, or a delicate cotton print.
- Rubber cement
- Stapler
- Scissors

Directions:
Cut the fabric two inches larger than the front of the book. Take the book apart to make handling easier. Cover book, folding over a generous hem. Glue or staple hem in place. Slit fabric above holes in the original cover. Place gummed reinforcements around each slit. To make your book even more precious, why not add pretty French paper, available in art supply stores, and tie it together with an embroidered ribbon?

With what will you fill your keepsake book? Try for the unusual. It's not the big things like baby's first step that you'll forget, but the everyday trivia. Include such items as the sheet of paper on which you recorded your contractions during labor. (Believe it or not, one of these days you'll enjoy reviewing it.)

You might also want to keep hospital souvenirs in your book—bracelets, pamphlets, schedules, doctor's written orders, etc. And by all means don't forget a delivery room picture, with baby all red and wet on top of Mama's tummy.

From here on out, your keepsake book becomes a long book of "firsts." A few ideas:
- Number of feedings during the first month
- Number of diaper changes during the first month
- Your first night of uninterrupted sleep
- Baby's first smile
- Baby's first coo
- Baby's first trip

You'll have many questions to ask the doctor, so write these questions as well as his answers in your book. They may come in handy next time around.

One busy mother never had time to complete memory books for her three children. But while each of them was still a baby, she sat down and wrote him a letter, all about how wonderful it was to be his mother and to hold him in her arms. I thought it was such a lovely idea, that I've included a space for you to do the same for your baby.

Dear Baby _____ ,

Much love,

_____

Kindness—
the art of loving

Christian women should be noticed for being kind and good, not for the way they fix their hair or because of their jewels or fancy clothes (1 Timothy 2:10, TLB).

During a visit to my parents' church, Mother introduced me to one of her friends. "Carolyn is so kind," she said to me later. "Actually, she's my inspiration. My life goal is to be as kind and good as this one woman."

Her statement sounded funny to me and I wondered why. Was it because I had never heard such a compliment before? Because I had never seen a woman kind enough to stand on her works alone? Or could it have been that I wasn't even sure what qualities determined kindness in a woman?

The Bible speaks often of Christian kindness, but I find a verse in Proverbs particularly helpful in guiding me, as a housewife, toward goals of kindness.

A gracious woman retaineth honour...
(Proverbs 11:16a).

Have you ever admired a certain woman's ability to take care of her guests? "She's such a gracious hostess," you find yourself saying with envy. And indeed she is, for this woman seems to be constantly at work, making sure that each person is comfortable, pleased with his refreshment, and having a good time.

All of us may not be accomplished hostesses, but we do try our best. Now just imagine treating your family with the same respect that you give your most honored guest, and you have a pretty good picture of kindness in action.

Kindness, you see, is little more than everyday graciousness—unceasing graciousness to all our fellowmen.

I find it no great surprise that we don't see an abundance of kindness today. In a day and age of "equal rights," kindness quite often comes across as unfair and too demanding. I can think of many times in my own life when a thoughtful gesture brought more feedback than I was willing to give and I complained, "You can't do anything nice for people nowadays without them wanting more." But does that really sound so unreasonable? For just as we look forward to returning to the gracious hostess' home, so we long for the comfort of a kind woman's love.

Christian women are wise to cultivate everyday graciousness because we have a permanent house guest—Jesus. And he deserves our company behavior, as does the family he has given us.

What is the Christian mother's best behavior? First of all, our best is sharing without complaint. Sharing, by the way, is more than sorting out a bunch of discarded clothing for the local charity drive. Sharing is giving that part of ourselves that really matters. It's giving your sick neighbor some of your freshly baked bread, even though it means you'll probably have to bake again for your own family the next day. It's putting another plate on the table, even though you've prepared something as indivisible as Cornish hens. It's making the sofa into a bed for a distraught friend, even though you've looked forward to an evening of solitude with Hubby. And it's taking the time to get down on the floor with your baby; even though you'd rather get the dishes done.

Second, our best is helping. But what

hard-working mother doesn't know about helping? A typical day for us includes a variety of service projects ranging from shoe-tying to phone-talking. We wipe noses, change diapers, prepare meals, and are always on hand for the extras such as birthday parties and last-minute outings. All of this—and yet because we're Christians there's more. After we're through at home, God expects us to seek out someone to help. That elderly woman on your block may need some assistance in housecleaning now and then. That young woman who struggles with children and packages on her walk home from the grocery store may need a lift in your car. And those people with whom you worship may be wrestling with all kinds of needs that you could help with. If you're like most mothers, you're wondering where you'll get the strength to take care of others in addition to your own. Don't let this simple matter discourage you, for God has promised to supply us with strength.

Our best also includes speaking kindly to one another. Think about your speech. Is it soft and loving, or harsh and commanding? It's interesting to note that children will always gravitate toward a kind woman no matter how large or foreign the crowd. Perhaps it's the voice that attracts them, for her gentle voice tells them that her words are sure to be kind. So, we as Christian mothers will want to raise our voices only on rare occasions and remember to use the courtesy words, please and thank you, even at home. Peter says it all in 1 Peter 4:11 when he tells us that whenever we speak it should be the voice or words of God.

Last of all, our best is treating others as we ourselves would like to be treated. I once had a third-grade teacher who was the epitome of kindness. When a student cried over a low test score, forgot his lunch money, or became ill during math, she was always ready to offer comfort without passing judgment. How could she be so understanding when other teachers would have lost their tempers? Simple. She remembered how it felt to be a third grader, and she treated each pupil with the thoughtfulness that she herself would have appreciated many years ago. Christian mothers can do the same. Consider how you want to be treated when you say the wrong thing, appear late or unprepared for a certain activity, or change your mind about a matter without enough cause—and treat others accordingly.

But maybe I'm making all of this sound too easy. It's not, you know. When a friend of mine insisted that she couldn't be kind because it just wasn't in her nature, I could only assure her that we all have the same problem. We are, after all, only human. It's sometimes easier to set simple goals of graciousness than to grow frustrated with our imperfections.

You might want to concentrate on merely speaking kindly of others for a few weeks. During this time, fill your thoughts with God. Scripture cards hung above the kitchen sink and on the bathroom mirror are invaluable for reminding you of your goal throughout the day. After you find *speaking* well of people easier, you're ready to start *doing* good for them. Every day will mark a new step in the growth of Christian love. Quoting Socrates, the Greek philosopher, Epictetus said:

One man finds pleasure in improving his land, another his horses; my pleasure lies in seeing that I myself grow better day by day.

And you will grow better. For the more we love one another, the wider the circle of love becomes. Kindness is steadfast love. It does require our best, but it is through giving our best that we are able to fulfill our responsibility to God and the people around us.

Language—
words of wisdom

"Habla español, amiga; no hables ingles."

"But how can I speak Spanish on the first day of class?" I questioned the teacher. And to myself I muttered angrily, "Why would I even be here if I already knew the language?"

I had selected Spanish to fill my foreign language requirement in college, and when the teacher announced that no English would be spoken for the duration of the course, I was frightened to death. That I could pass such a course seemed an impossibility, but as the semester wore on, rules relaxed and the more difficult lessons were often explained in English.

It was then that I first realized what a remarkable feat talking is for the infant. After all, there is never a time when rules can relax enough to allow an adult to speak the babbles of babyhood. Baby must simply persist.

Experts tell us that mothers have a natural gift for teaching speech. Even without special knowledge, a mother guides her baby toward the world of language. And it all begins with that first coo. Mother smiles with delight at this tiny sound and coos back in imitation. Baby thinks this is a lovely game and an even lovelier way to win a twinkle from Mom's eye.

Soon he says a sound that resembles a word in the tiniest way, and it becomes a household word. "Give him his ba," Mom orders Dad. And bingo! Baby has discovered the power of communication.

Now, he must learn the secrets of this wonderful thing called talking, and during his busy day of learning he takes time for watching others make those all-important sounds. Baby notices the shape of their mouths, the placement of their tongues, even the muscles in their necks. And he practices and practices and practices on any sound that he can happen upon as he babbles. When we hear these musical sounds early in the morning, we say he's playing quietly in his bed—actually, he's working, and diligently, too.

Left solely in the hands of nature, babies do an amazing job of learning to talk. But when parents help, things go so much faster, and learning becomes a fun game for everyone involved. I once knew a speech teacher who taught her daughter to speak at the age of nine months. While most of us have neither the patience nor the know-how to tackle such a project, we still want to do our part. As a mother you're in a prime position for teaching speech; as a Christian, you face a grave responsibility. Someday, that baby you're holding may have to tell another about Jesus.

A MOTHER'S TEN COMMANDMENTS FOR TEACHING SPEECH

1. Speak clearly and slowly at all times. This gives the baby a chance to catch and isolate certain sounds. When you're talking directly to him try exaggerating the shape of your mouth once in a while and remember to put end consonants on words that end with the letters t, d, etc. As for baby talk, suit yourself. I used to think parents who conversed in this ridiculous language, just that—ridiculous. Now I'm not so quick to judge. For one thing, the children of these parents learn to talk just like everyone else. And for another, it's hard to resist a little goochy-goochy when you're cuddling a newborn.

2. Face your baby when talking to him. He wants and needs to see the body language that accompanies speech. In fact, you'll find that unless the young baby sees your face, your words sometimes carry no meaning. And of course, as I said earlier, the actual production of sound is boosted by his imitating your mouth shape.

3. Never push your baby in his speaking efforts. While it's probably true that early speech is a sign of intelligence, it shouldn't be used as conclusive evidence one way or the other. Einstein, by the way, didn't talk until he was three years old.

4. Repeat words when talking to the baby. Repetition is an old but proven teaching method that works as well in talking as in anything else.

5. Give all objects a name. For instance, when you're powdering the baby, say the word "powder" aloud and hold the can where he can see it. You can do the same with shoes, socks, spoons, and toys.

6. Listen to your baby's language—foreign as it may be. Let your face show that what he says is important. If you don't give him this courtesy, he's likely to give up with a "what's the use" attitude. Besides, the sooner the baby learns that listening is part of communication, the easier your life will be.

7. Never leave your baby in the care of someone who speaks poorly. This can be a problem when we're depending on the inexpen-

sive child-care services of foreigners or very uneducated people. Certainly, I'm not suggesting that these people are not good enough for us; we're all equal in God's eyes. But I am saying that your child will imitate the speech of whomever he spends the most time with. If for some reason you must spend a great deal of time away from home, use the utmost care in selecting a baby-sitter.

8. Encourage the educational television shows. Children shows such as *Sesame Street*, *Mr. Rodgers*, and *Electric Company* fascinate even the very young baby and are great vocabulary builders. He'll be especially happy if you take the time to watch these shows with him.

9. Keep your speech free of profanity. Hopefully, this is not a problem with Christian mothers. Sometimes, however, motherhood finds us struggling with unattractive habits acquired in our own childhood. Cursing never sounded worse than from the mouth of an innocent child; maybe the very thought of it will be enough to persuade us to tidy up that speech.

10. Speak in a pleasant, friendly manner. Sarcasm, nagging, and complaining will produce a whiny, irritable child, and it certainly doesn't help the home atmosphere either.

TALKING GAMES

1. Experiment with sounds as you play with your baby. Copy the baby's sounds and then make up a new sound for him to copy. You may discover that he doesn't even attempt this sound until days later. (Perhaps he's practicing in private.)

2. When the baby is around nine months old, make him an alphabet sound book. You can draw the letter and illustrate it with a picture that explains the sound. Example: "Sammy the snake makes *Sssss* sounds in the grass." Try reading to baby during mealtime. It provides you a captive audience and makes his dinner more interesting.

3. Name each object as you dress the baby. Example: "Now let's put on your sock." (Hold up sock.)

4. Play the question game. Example: "Where is Baby's shoe?" (Hold up shoe.) "Here is Baby's shoe."

5. Hang a mirror knee level to you on a wall in the baby's room. Sitting in front of it, show baby how to watch himself make different sounds.

PROGRESS CHART—but not all babies will do these things at the same age!

2 months—baby will coo
9 months—baby will say DaDa
10 months—baby will say MaMa
1 year—baby will speak single words
2 years—baby will speak in simple sentences

Layette—size 0

Infant dresses—half price!

As I read this sale sign in a large department store, a rather overweight woman leaned across the table of baby clothing and said, "Honey, you might as well buy two. The way I look at it, we only wear size 0 once in a lifetime."

Glancing into my daughter's crowded closet

would have been enough to convince anyone that I shared this woman's philosophy. But I didn't and I don't. How did all those clothes get there? I only wish I knew. And you may be asking yourself this same question several months from now, because if there's one thing that Americans have in common, it's the habit of overindulgence. We lean subconsciously toward the extravagant, and when it comes to our children, I'm afraid we're at our worst.

But who can blame us? With so many wonderful baby products on the markets, it really does simplify things to just "take all."

Even practical people find themselves exchanging their own rules for those of the fashionable baby books and begin checking off items from extensive lists. One of these lists is below.

You might want to try one or two of each item, but be careful about purchasing the recommended quantity. The first month of parenthood will determine those articles you like best and want more of. Do remember that while the number of garments you'll need for the baby will depend on your washing situation, the style of these garments is a matter of taste.

6 nightgowns
6 shirts
6 sacques
6 kimonos
6 stretch suits
1 sweater
1 bonnet
1 pair booties
4 dozen diapers
1 bunting
4 plastic pants
2 sets of diaper pins
4 bibs
6 receiving blankets
4 blankets
3 lap pads
6 sheets
6 bath towels
6 washcloths

A CLOSER LOOK

Gowns. Long gowns make comfortable sleeping gear. They usually come in polyester blends, but if you can find 100 percent cotton gowns at a garage sale or in a friend's attic, grab them. Cotton nightclothes launder better than their modern counterparts in spite of their age. The mittens that are attached to these gowns are designed to keep little hands warm, and the drawstring bottom can't be beat for swaddling your newborn.

T-Shirts. T-shirts come in a wide assortment of styles: pull-overs, snap-closing fronts, and tie-closing fronts. They come in delicate prints with pants to match, display colors as bright as the sun, and sport sayings equally as bold. Crafty mothers even add glamor to those dull white ones with lovely embroidery and appliques. Short shirts are good daytime wear for a baby. Like the nightgowns, they are made of soft blends and keep wet clothing to a minimum. Start with the six-month size; these shirts run small regardless of the quality.

Sacques and kimonos. These are nothing

more than little shirts or gowns worn over a baby's dress or diaper shirt for a dressier appearance. They are usually made of satins and lace.

Stretch suits. Many people favor these little sleeperlike suits for both day and night. They have snap closings that run from the neck down one or both legs, and I found them a bit messy to work with after a breastfed infant's bowel movement. You may not agree.

Sweaters. Beautiful sweater sets with bonnet and booties are a popular shower gift, but if you haven't received one, let the season be your guide. A baby born in midsummer in one of our Southern states probably doesn't need an elaborate sweater set. On the other hand, my daughter was still wearing some of her infant sweaters when she was a year old. The sleeves hit her arms about elbow length, and they looked like little jackets. So, with a bit of experimenting, nothing need be wasted.

Bonnet. Here again, a cotton hat or bonnet may be more practical for the summer baby.

Booties. It's a rare baby who only owns one pair of booties. Although those pretty crocheted booties make lovely gifts, you'll find yourself going back for more of the ordinary stocking booties that can't be kicked off.

Bunting. Why some women prefer to go to extremes in wrapping baby up for his winter outings is beyond me. If a bunting is purchased with your area's weather in mind, you need only pop baby into it and be on your way.

Plastic pants. A newborn baby wets so lightly that you can easily get by with only one or two pairs of plastic pants until baby is close to four months old. Use these pants sparingly during hot months to avoid diaper rash.

Blankets. Lightweight flannel blankets are great for keeping baby comfortable inside the house. Some mothers use them to dry the baby after his bath. You'll also want a few quilts or regular baby blankets. Today's thermal blankets are quick drying, good for year-round weather, and a favorite among young children.

Lap pads. If you decide against plastic pants during the early months, you'll need a generous supply of lap pads.

Sheets. Books almost always recommend purchasing more sheets than you'll ever need. Even mothers without washing machines usually can manage just fine with only three sets.

Bath towels. Special baby towels are nice gifts to receive. But before you waste money on any yourself, check your linen closet. A soft towel will do fine.

Washcloths. Small, soft washcloths are such a minor expense and such a functional piece of equipment that I'd encourage you to splurge and buy as many as ten. You'll still be using them two years from now.

Bibs. Directions for making a bib are at the end of this chapter. These bibs are inexpensive and everlasting.

Creepers. By the time baby is six months old, he'll begin to kick off his covers at night and you'll need to compensate. Pajamas with feet in them are an old-time remedy. Pay more for quality and use them on a second child.

Overalls or leotards. When your little one starts crawling, you'll want to protect his knees with overalls or leotards—whichever is appropriate. Choose overalls with snaps running down both legs for easy diaper changes.

Shoes. Until baby starts walking, you needn't worry about shoes. At that point, he should be taken to a shoe store for a professional fit.

Dress-up clothes. A baby should have at least two sets of dress-up clothes. If he's lucky enough to have more, remember to dress him up just for your own pleasure once in a while. It'll make you an even happier mother.

As you can see, there's really not that much to choosing baby's clothing. Keeping him clean and comfortable covers the subject in more ways than one.

80   LAYETTE

LAYETTE

CUTTING LINE

BIB INSTRUCTIONS

Materials needed:
  1 washcloth
  1 packet bias tape

Instructions for sewing: Fold and cut bib as indicated by pattern. Pin bias tape to neck opening. Sew in place. Cut two strips of bias tape 7 inches long. Run seam down middle of each strip of tape. Sew one strip on each side of neck opening for ties.

Variations:
1. Hand towel bibs are larger versions of the above and are especially nice for the older baby.
2. Instead of bias tape, you can close neck opening with gripper snaps or Velcro fastener.
3. Decorate your bibs with appliques, lace, and embroidery.

FOLD

Lengthen 2½" here

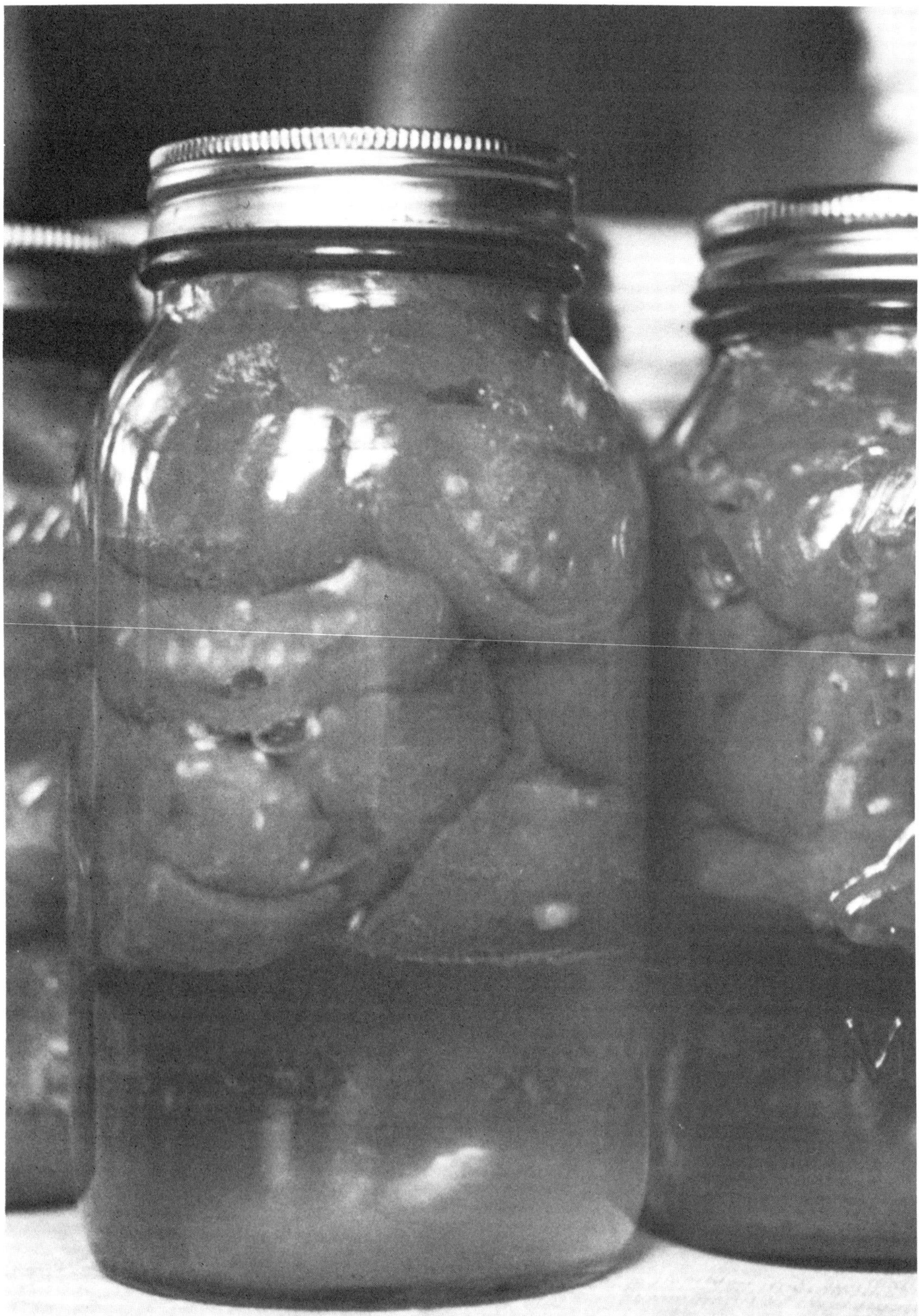

Meal planning—minute menus

Better is a dinner of herbs where love is, than a stalled ox and hatred therewith (Proverbs 15:17).

It's not surprising that mothers often feel their worst at dinnertime. We race through the day cleaning house, chasing children, attending meetings—seldom taking time to eat, rest, or exercise properly ourselves. Come evening, when there's a meal to prepare, a baby to calm, and a husband to greet, our bodies cop out with fatigue, and you can guess what happens to dinner.

We usually become interested in nutrition for the first time during our pregnancy. Later, as we watch our baby grow and develop with the help of our breast milk, we really begin to think twice about food value. A wholesome, well-balanced diet on the dinner table becomes a top intellectual priority which, unfortunately, doesn't always materialize.

A lot of mothers have solved the dinnertime dilemma with fancy microwave ovens; others have stocked their freezers with costly frozen goods. And some of us, who believe in eating healthful foods as close to their natural state as possible, actually get by with neither. Our secret? Simple, no-fuss menus that take only minutes of preparation time.

Take vegetables, for instance. There's no need to rely on canned or frozen vegetables when it is much easier to serve them raw. Broccoli, cauliflower, zucchini, carrots, and cabbage are only a few of the typically cooked vegetables that lend themselves well to a salad. Or, you might try serving these vegetables with a sour cream dip as an appetizer. Use a stainless steel scrubber to make the cleaning easy and quick. Besides serving more nutrition this way, you'll save yourself from having to clean a dirty pan.

Among the vegetables that we do like to serve cooked, potatoes rank high as a family favorite. They can be popped into the oven with nothing but a washing, or chopped into quarters and cooked in their jackets on top of the stove. Never, however, overcook your vegetables. Bring them to a boil and then reduce the heat so that you'll lose fewer of those valuable nutrients.

And then there's meat. I wonder how many of us mothers are guilty of quickly producing a pan of breaded fish sticks at dinnertime? What a shame, when the real thing only takes seconds under the broiler. You can also cut down on fuss by cooking meat and fowl overnight at a low temperature in your oven or slow cooker. Go ahead and choose those larger cuts of meat, and you'll have enough left over for lunches the next day. This is a good way to eliminate one more chore and assure a nursing mother and active toddler a good midday meal.

Meat doesn't always have to provide the protein, though; egg and cheese dishes are welcome changes at anyone's house. And of course, you won't want to overlook beans. Here's a protein-packed food that cooks slowly all afternoon, leaving you free to care for baby. (If you soak beans overnight, retain the vitamins by cooking them in the soaking water.) For a real emergency or simply a little variation, you can feed your family nutritiously from a snack table of nuts, cheese, fresh fruit, and whole-wheat bread.

As for desserts, your energy shouldn't be wasted on preparing fancy confections. A bowl of fresh fruit compliments any meal. But when you must satisfy a sweet tooth, and we all must occasionally, serve puddings as they do have more food value than other sweets.

Below are a few of my favorite "hassle free" recipes. You'll notice that they can all be prepared in their aluminum foil packets early in the day and stored in the refrigerator until cooking time. While dinner is simmering, you have only to get yourself together. Try a glass of orange juice mixed with one tablespoon brewers yeast. This pickup will take about twenty minutes to go into effect, so in the meantime, why not lie down to nurse the baby before setting the table.

Dinner may be hours away yet, but the sight of a set table will calm your hungry husband. For as long as there are small children around, it may never be easy to prepare the evening meal. But if you follow the rules of simple, nutritious eating, dinnertime won't be the most difficult part of your day.

BAR-B-Q CHICKEN

4 T. butter
1 T. brown sugar
½ cup chopped onion

1 tsp. vinegar
2 T. Worcestershire sauce
¼ cup lemon juice
¾ cup ketchup
2 lbs. chicken parts

Combine first 7 ingredients in sauce pan. Bring to boil. Reduce heat, simmer 15 minutes.
Rub chicken with salt and pepper and place on large sheet of foil. Pour sauce over chicken. Seal foil. Bake at 350° for one hour.

HAMBURGER LOAF

1 lb. ground beef
1 egg
1/3 cup milk
½ slice bread (crumbled)
1 small onion (chopped fine)
1 tsp. salt
¼ tsp. pepper
1 T. steak sauce
½ T. prepared mustard
1 loaf Italian bread, split lengthwise
8 pieces of cheddar cheese

Mix first 9 ingredients. Place bottom half of bread loaf on large piece of foil. Spread meat mixture on bread. Seal foil. Bake at 350° for one hour. Open foil, place cheese slices on top of meat. Return to oven with foil open until cheese melts. Save top half of bread to eat with spaghetti the next day.

FOIL ROAST

4 lbs. chuck roast
1 envelope dry onion soup mix
1 oz. can sliced mushrooms (juice drained) or
  ½ cup fresh mushrooms thinly sliced

Place meat in center of large piece of foil. Sprinkle with soup mix and mushrooms. Seal foil. Bake at 350° for 2½ to 3 hours or until meat is tender.

CHICKEN SPECIAL

2 lbs. chicken parts
1 can cream of chicken soup
1 cup cooked green beans
4 medium potatoes (peeled and quartered)
salt and pepper to taste

Wrap chicken, soup, beans and potatoes in foil. (If using canned vegetables, drain liquid.) Bake at 350° for one hour.

Mistakes— when mom goofs up

Imagine a nurse accidentally giving you the wrong medication. Even worse, imagine yourself as that nurse. Impossible? Maybe, and then again, maybe not. I once knew someone who made such a mistake. She was an intelligent, sensitive, highly competent worker. She was well-liked by her fellow staff, trusted by her boss, and adored by the patients. But even so, she made the mistake.

Luckily, this woman was surrounded by a great deal of love. She underwent no loss of job, no severe reprimand, and scarcely any teasing. But there was pain, nonetheless. I watched her suffer for a good year as the guilt slowly worked itself out.

Mothers make many mistakes, and you won't be any exception. There'll be times when you yell angrily at your baby, only to recognize too late that it was something he didn't deserve. There'll be times when you leave a suspiciously flushed-looking child with the baby-sitter, only to return to a feverish sick one. There'll be times when you insist on a certain behavior, only to realize later that it was obviously the wrong route to take. Mistakes like these are all a part of motherhood. You may not make the same blunders that I have made, but you'll make your own. And learning how to handle these "wrong moves" can make your job of mothering a little bit easier.

I've often wondered just why mistakes make us feel so wretched. It's probably because they remind us that we've fallen short of a particular goal. Remember when you carried that baby inside of you and you vowed you'd never get angry at the darling? Now you've broken that vow in one short second. Besides filling you with an inconsolable disappointment in yourself, mistakes like this leave you with an immense sense of guilt. It's typical to wonder if there wasn't something we could have done to avoid our actions, and to question ourselves as to whether or not we gave our best to that situation. Battling with such negative thoughts results in a physically fatigued and emotionally drained mother, and brings the very worst of our human qualities into play. And who should get hit, but our dear family.

We can't always avoid mistakes, but perhaps a careful look at your life style will help you cut down on the number you make. Most mothers can profit a great deal by simply slowing down. Take a look at your daily routine. If it involves gardening, elaborate cooking, outings, and entertaining in addition to mothering—you need a break. What's the big rush, anyway? If we truly believe in eternal life, there's plenty of time for everything. Now is the time for being a mother; later is the time for being a doer.

You might be surprised at the mistakes you *don't* make when your life becomes uncluttered. As for those things you can't cut out, maybe the most difficult tasks need to be moved to that time of day when you're at your best. Or perhaps a little organization could help minimize last-minute confusion that ultimately leads to mistakes (missing diaper bags, checkbooks, and car keys have contributed to far more than their share of mishaps).

Some women find that learning to say "no" to time-consuming projects gives them a new, relaxed outlook on life that helps them to do their daily chores with more competence. Others claim that taking their phone off the hook during peak pressure hours saves them from energy-draining frustration. Of course, you needn't strive for the title "efficiency expert." Just try to live peacefully, unselfishly, and slowly. Life goes on forever and ever when we believe in God.

About those mistakes that we do make—Christian mothers need to overcome them and move on. Start with admitting that you made a mistake, and apologize. If there's something that you can do to make things right, do it. Chances are, there won't be, and that's exactly what makes a mistake so difficult to bear. We have to accept it and forgive ourselves. In the end, we have only to answer to God; he will forgive and so we must do the same. When

---

He that is without sin among you, let him first cast a stone (John 8:7).

all is said and done, punishing yourself will only lead to punishing those around you, which your family doesn't deserve, and neither do you.

Is it so hard to admit that we're human? There isn't a man on earth who doesn't make mistakes; you and I are no different.

Mistakes can even be a terrific opportunity for learning. After you've made that wrong move, quickly review the situation for weak spots that can be corrected next time. If you find none, simply forget the whole issue. Unexplained cooking, sewing, and craft mistakes often indicate nothing more than poor instruction. If the mistake was due to an obvious error on your part, say to yourself, "Now I know it doesn't work that way." (You've just admitted to learning something.)

Each of us must bear some faults and burdens of his own. For none of us is perfect! (Galatians 6:5, TLB).

Try separating yourself from what you do. Regardless of how terrible the blunder, you're still the same worthwhile person that you always were. Sure, it's upsetting when we don't achieve those things that we wanted to. But as long as we've put forth our best, God has allowed us to reach the ultimate of our abilities in that particular area. It might help to remember that we are, after all, only instruments of God. We can't claim success as our own, and likewise, God doesn't expect us to take the blame for all the things that go wrong. He does, however, ask us to accept our share of imperfections with grace.

Being able to acknowledge your mistake with a simply statement such as, "Yes, I made a mistake," is another therapeutic action. And besides, it's tremendous evidence of maturity. Sometimes it helps to laugh about the incident. Certainly this is not appropriate behavior immediately after a serious mistake, but later on you can share the story with a touch of humor. Hearing others laugh with you will turn a catastrophe into fond memories.

Have you learned to recognize a mistake? A lot of people accuse themselves of mistakes that could be better classified as poor choices. For instance, I once talked to a woman who said, "The one mistake I made was giving my baby a juice bottle."

But, come now. Was this really a mistake? It sounded more like a choice to me. The mother had *chosen* to feed her baby juices from a bottle. Maybe with the next child she will indeed decide upon a different feeding method, but her new choice may not be any better. Life is full of choices, and just because we decide that we don't like a certain choice doesn't make it a mistake.

Last of all, don't despair over your mistakes. God has a way of turning disaster into beauty. A burned dinner can often mean an evening out. An uncorrectable sewing mistake adds exotic scraps to your craft basket. And it's not unusual for a mistake to open doors by prompting us to develop a new procedure, or helping us decide upon more training. But the most perfect example of this beauty is the unexpected baby who is thought of as a mistake during pregnancy and a joy after birth. Of course, none of us will ever feel good about making a mistake. So, when you do make one, remember to look at the horizon. There will always be a rainbow and a reason to move on.

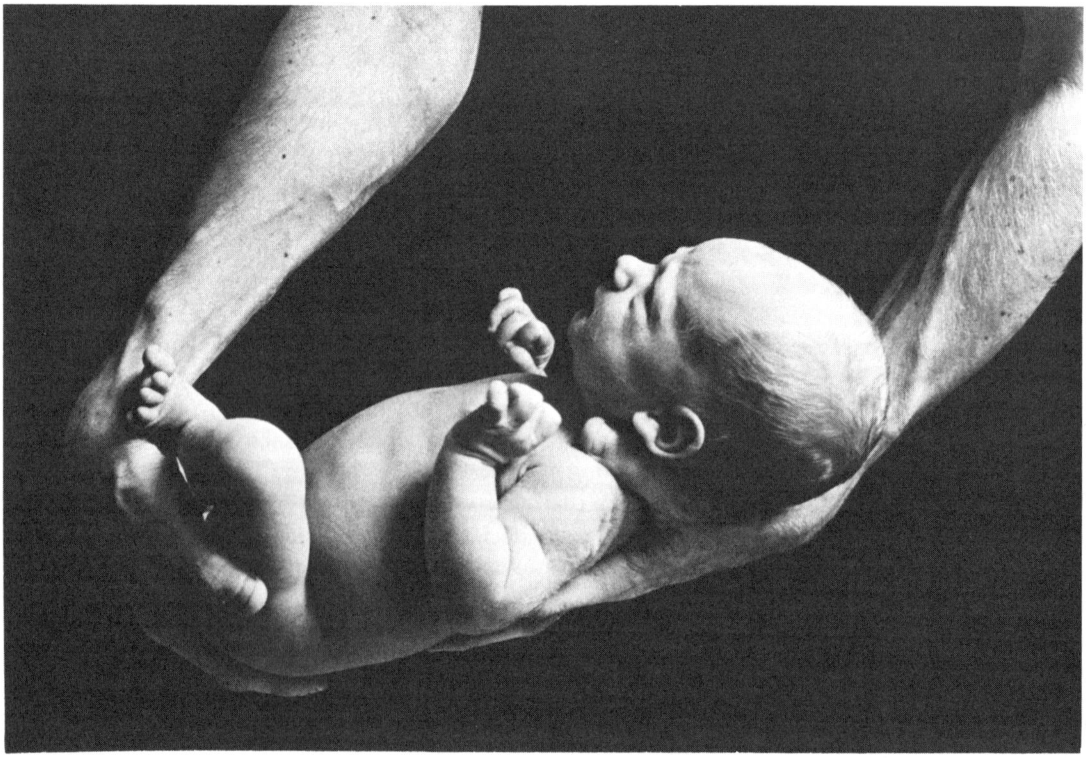

Natural childbirth—all things considered

No matter what the procedure, birth is a normal, natural process for the female. Because of this, I have divided natural childbirth into three categories—prepared childbirth, anesthetized childbirth, and operative childbirth. (A rather detailed account of the caesarean section is included because women who give birth in this way often complain of few resources to turn to.) The type of delivery that you will have will depend largely on what you desire in the way of a birth experience and what will ultimately produce a healthy baby and mother.

PREPARING FOR PARENTHOOD (PREPARED CHILDBIRTH)

I'm beginning to think that more people are prepared for giving birth these days than not,

It seems to be the trend to take classes in labor and delivery techniques, even for those who have no intentions of "going it on their own." Still, we do have people who either pursue or avoid this experience purely due to lack of information. To help you decide for yourself, here are ten frequently asked questions about prepared childbirth.

1. What is prepared childbirth?

Prepared childbirth is training for the physical and mental control of a normal labor and delivery.

2. What are the advantages of prepared childbirth?

The most commonly quoted advantages of prepared childbirth are:

   a. The mother goes into labor with an understanding of the birth process and the ability to cooperate with her body as it goes through the various stages of labor.
   b. The mother's muscles have been prepared to work effectively during labor and delivery.
   c. Although analgesics are sometimes used, anesthesia is not routinely used within a normal prepared childbirth experience. The absence of drugs means a safer delivery for the baby.
   d. During a prepared childbirth, the father becomes more than a helpless bystander. He is, in fact, the pillar of strength behind it all.

3. What exactly is involved in preparing for labor and delivery?

With the help of your husband, you will be preparing for the hardest work that you will ever do in your life. It will therefore require a great deal of cooperation and willingness to learn on the part of both of you. The instructors will attempt to thoroughly educate you in all areas of childbirth, but you will be expected to supplement their knowledge with a recommended reading list and to practice the various exercises each day until birth. This in itself really takes willpower, because the expectant mother is chronically tired, and the expectant father is often so busy that he's not easily pinned down. Suffice it to say that you're in for a lot of rewarding but *hard* work.

4. Does prepared childbirth guarantee the absence of pain?

Because fear seems to contribute to and intensify pain, women who are knowledgeable of the childbirth process often experience little or no pain. It should be noted, however, that some women have a higher pain threshold than others. If you do experience discomfort during birth, it isn't a sign that prepared childbirth or you, yourself, have failed in any way.

5. How can prepared childbirth benefit the woman who is anesthetized during delivery?

First of all, going into labor with a working knowledge of what to expect can't help but be reassuring to the mother. Then, too, as most hospitals do allow Dad in the labor room regardless of the birth procedure, it only makes sense for him to be capable of coaching, encouraging, and even aiding his wife with simple nursing procedures. Second, prepared childbirth instruction will teach you exercises that will tone the muscles used in labor and delivery and help you relax during the contractions of labor. Many mothers who have delivered their babies by caesarean section claim that these exercises left them in such good physical condition that they recovered faster than was expected of them.

6. How long is the average labor in a prepared childbirth situation?

Although some women experience a quick three-hour delivery, an eight- to twelve-hour labor is quite normal for a first baby. Each successive child will generally come much faster. But regardless of the length of your labor, you can expect to exert the same amount of physical energy.

7. To what extent does the father help in a prepared childbirth?

The father is the best labor coach there is. He reduces anxiety by being continuously on hand throughout labor. He offers encouragement, supervises exercises, times contractions, and actually administers physical aid to the mother via backrubs, hot compresses, ice chips, etc. Most hospitals allow the prepared father into the delivery room where he continues to give encouragement and support. At no time, however, does he interfere with the delivery of the baby; this is the physician's job.

8. Is an episiotomy necessary in the prepared childbirth situation?

An episiotomy, which is an incision at the opening of the vagina, is usually performed just prior to delivery of the baby's head so that it will not tear the perineum. In a very quick and uncomplicated delivery, this procedure may be omitted. But this is not the normal practice, as most doctors feel that the potential damage to the perineum or vagina makes it not worth foregoing an episiotomy.

9. Must the mother who delivers in a hospital spend some time in the recovery room?

You can probably expect to remain in recovery for at least a couple of hours. In this room there will always be qualified personnel available to give you prompt attention should complications arise. Of course, if you're to have rooming-in, you'll be impatient to be with your baby, but try to relax and rest—you've earned it.

Because your physician plays such an important part in a prepared childbirth, you need to inquire about the classes during your first prenatal visit. If he is unfamiliar and unwilling to participate in this type of delivery, contact the local hospital. They will be able to give you the names of doctors who support prepared childbirth.

A TRADITIONAL TRIUMPH (THE ANESTHETIZED BIRTH)

You may have no desire to experience birth without some form of anesthesia. And in the case of a difficult or operative birth, you may have no choice but to be anesthetized. To help you understand the various types of anesthetics available, here is a simple glossary. Do note, however, that since anesthetics are within your doctor's realm, I am leaving the details to be explained by him.

General anesthesia. Puts the mother completely to sleep. Pentothal and/or gas is usually used to attain this relaxed state, just prior to birth. There is little if any side-effect on the mother and it is safe for the baby too.

Regional anesthesia. Takes away all sensation in the anesthetized area. The mother is fully awake and able to cooperate; and of all anesthetics, regional has the least effect on the baby. Some common methods of regional anesthesia are the caudal, the spinal, the epidural, and the cervical block. If you are planning on regional anesthesia, discuss this matter with your doctor early in your pregnancy as every doctor seems to have his favorite method and each method varies a little.

Local anesthesia. Is occasionally used in the prepared childbirth procedure. It involves nothing more than injecting novocaine or a similar drug in the vaginal area just prior to delivery. Another name for this is the pudental block.

SPECIAL DELIVERY (THE CAESAREAN SECTION)

I once worked for a doctor who claimed that the only truly beautiful newborn babies were those delivered by caesarean section. "They're the only ones that don't look as if they've been squeezed through a keyhole," he argued with us women who insisted that all newborn babies were beautiful.

And in a sense, he was right, for when we gaze into the nursery window, that lovely infant with the perfectly rounded head and soft pink skin is more often than not a c-section baby. This is the baby who, instead of having made his entrance into the world in the conventional way, arrived via an incision in his mother's abdominal wall and uterus.

A caesarean section, although considered by experts to be a simple operation, is nevertheless major abdominal surgery, and the decision to do it requires the best of medical judgment— it's never an elective on the mother's part. One of the most common reasons for performing a caesarean section is cephalopelvic disproportion, which simply means that the mother's bony pelvis is too small for an average-size baby to be delivered vaginally. This situation can also include a mother whose pelvis is average in size but whose baby is large. Other reasons for this type of surgery are placenta previa, a condition in which the placenta is attached low down in the cervix region rather than high up on the interior wall of the uterus; premature separation of the placenta from the uterus; the breech position of a baby; and uterine inertia, the term used to describe unusually weak contractions of the uterus.

Sometimes it's necessary for the doctor to perform an emergency caesarean section. This may happen when the pelvic disproportion is questionable, and the decision for a c-section can't be made without a trial of labor; or when there is any other reason to believe that to allow labor to continue would endanger the life of the baby. These situations don't arise often enough to justify worry on your part, but it seems that an emergency c-section always catches the mother off guard, and the sudden change of events becomes not only disappointing but perplexing. More than one woman has rather wistfully remarked that if she had only been as well informed of the c-section delivery as she had been of a normal delivery, her birth experience could have been much happier.

So, what exactly should be expected, if you should be scheduled for a caesarean section, or if your delivery quite suddenly doesn't go as planned and the decision for a caesarean section is made?

First of all, because a c-section is major surgery, you'll be treated like a pre- and postoperative patient. Since procedures vary, it would be a good idea to ask your doctor what to expect, but if there isn't time for a discussion, cooperate with the nurses who have been instructed to prep you. The procedure usually involves a stomach shave and catheterization in addition to the routine maternity prep that you might have received earlier.

Almost any anesthesia can be used. Regional anesthesia is often chosen because it has the least effect upon the baby, but occasionally in an emergency situation you must take what is quickest and most readily available. And sometimes, to the mother's dismay, this is general anesthesia. This is often a letdown to the woman who has dreamed of being awake during the birth of her baby. But if this should happen to you, don't argue with your doctor. He will, throughout the procedure, be doing only what is best for you and your baby.

The surgery itself takes about an hour, but your husband will have the joy of seeing the baby only minutes after you've been wheeled into the operating room. The incision is made either vertically or horizontally and is approximately six inches long. The doctor delivers the baby and placenta and then sews you back up.

How you feel after surgery will depend upon the individual situation. You'll spend somewhere around twelve hours after surgery in the recovery room, during which time your

vital signs will be checked periodically.
A moderate amount of discomfort is usually expected to last for about forty-eight hours, but analgesics do a marvelous job of controlling it. Throughout the next few days, regular postoperative measures will be taken. Intravenous fluids are often given, oral intake is measured, and urine output is either measured in a special container or taken care of by catheterization. Some doctors will even have you up and walking in the hall as soon as the special procedures have been stopped.

By the third day, you'll feel well enough to have your baby rooming-in, if your doctor and hospital permit. Perhaps solids will be offered to you at this time, but you may be surprised to discover that steak and potatoes aren't as appealing as you thought they'd be. It might take a while for your appetite, urination, and bowel movements to return to normal; but before you know it, the usual three- to seven-day hospital stay will be over.

No doubt about it, having a baby by way of major surgery isn't the easiest method of childbirth. But of all the operations that can be performed, it's surely one of the most fulfilling.

Hints for the Caesarean-Section Mother.

1. Do continue with your plans for nursing the baby, if such is the case. Nursing your baby stimulates the uterus to contract and prevents hemorrhage. Besides, it's a great emotional comfort to the postoperative mother.

2. Request a private room, even if rooming-in isn't available. You'll need more quiet and rest than the other mothers in the maternity wing.

3. To help you feel better the first day or two after delivery, move from side to side as much as possible, drink plenty of fluids, and breathe deeply several times a day.

4. When not feeding the baby, sleep. Those books, television programs, and phone conversations will still be interesting when you're more fully recovered.

5. Remind the nurses of your needs whenever necessary. They are there to help you, and proper medical care is one of the things that you'll be paying for.

6. Before leaving the hospital, have your husband do the following:
   a. Arrange for house help
   b. Stock the pantry
   c. Set up a card table beside your bed and place a nightlight and a rocker in your bedroom
   d. Discourage visitors

7. Remember that all new mothers recuperate at different speeds. Some women swear that their convalescent period after a c-section was very brief, while others admit that it was a good three months before they felt really well again. Just do the best you can. The discomfort and long recovery that a c-section mother must submit to often give her an overwhelming amount of patience and tenderness in caring for her baby.

Nursing— a new look at an old art

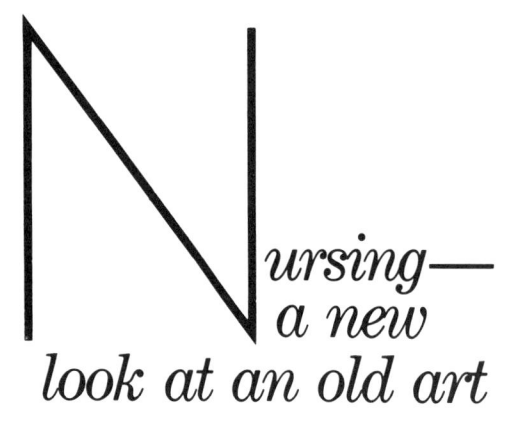

Dr. Niles Newton, who is so well known for her *Family Book of Child Care*, once said that there are basically two types of women—those who breastfeed and those who don't. She claims that those who do are generally more maternal, warmer, more loving, more satisfied with their natural role as mothers and women. Breathes there a Christian woman on earth who doesn't want a part of that kind of mothering?

We've made wonderful advances in the development of infant feeding. Chemists and physicians now tell us that today's formula is *almost* as good for baby as breast milk. Even pediatricians, whose best interest is always the child, sometimes tell prospective mothers, "Do what you want." Nursing a baby, they say, is far too complicated an endeavor to enter into halfheartedly. And I couldn't agree more. Still, there are those women who just aren't sure. They like the idea of breastfeeding, and are quick to admit that they want the advantages that breastfeeding offers baby, and yet, for little more than a song and a dance, they'd give it all up in the name of freedom. But before you decide against breastfeeding take a close look at the bottlefeeding mother. Watch her as she prepares formula each day. Watch her as she packs her diaper bag with bottles, nipples, and formulas. And watch her as she struggles with her fretful infant between feedings. This is freedom?

People who have never nursed sometimes assume that the satisfaction of nursing is knowing you're giving the best to your baby. And while it's true that breastfeeding means fewer illnesses and allergies for baby, it's really a great deal more than that. Breastfeeding is a whole way of mothering, I've heard it referred to as the third and completing phase of the maternity cycle. First, there's pregnancy—when you're in love with the very idea of a baby—any baby. Next, there's birth, when you meet your infant and experience "love at first sight." And then, there's nursing, when the two of you are practically one and as "batty" over each other as any newfound lovers. This special bond between nursing mothers and their infants is probably one of the best known emotional advantages of breastfeeding. Midnight feedings and colicky babies may tire the nursing mother, but they don't seem to leave her with the same burned-out thoughts on motherhood that are so commonly found among bottlefeeding mothers under similar strain. What causes the physical and spiritual ties between a breastfeeding mother and her infant? Experts tell us that it is probably due to a physiological factor, for the release of the hormone, prolactin, during lactation seems to contribute to motherly instinct. And then, too, both baby and mother have something that the other needs. Baby needs his mother's milk, and mother needs the physical relief that comes when baby takes her milk. Such give and take is a natural part of a relationship of love.

Give, and it shall be given unto you... (Luke 6:38a).

If there is any situation in life for which these words don't hold true—I have yet to discover it. Certainly breastfeeding is no exception. Mother gives freely and unselfishly of herself and reaps unimaginable blessings in return. For starters, there's convenience. Breast milk is readily available; thus, no waiting for the milk to warm while your infant cries from hunger. Then, of course, breastfeeding fits so easily and naturally into family life. For instance, although you'll want to drop everything just to nurse baby every once in a while, the nice thing is, you don't have to. Mom can be doing anything from reading with a younger child to enjoying dinner with hubby—all while feeding her baby. And as for going out, what could be easier than toting along a breastfed infant? A couple of spare diapers and your own good milk is all you need to keep your baby happy.

Maybe another reason that nursing mothers seem so content in their maternal role is that they regain their pre-pregnancy figure so quickly. During and after each feeding, the hormone oxytocin causes the uterus to contract and actually return to its normal size faster than it would if the mother didn't nurse. Even those extra pounds accumulated during pregnancy present few problems because making milk burns up calories more pleasantly than any diet.

Last, but not least, is the simple pleasure derived from nursing. This aspect of breastfeeding is not easily understood by anyone who has not nursed; yet it is freely admitted to by those who have. Breastfeeding is not like a sexual release, but it is very much a sensual experience. Women will often speak of having a "physical high" while nursing their babies, and while we could spend all day analyzing this sensation, one woman summed up my feelings when she said, "God thinks of everything!" Exactly. If this pleasure were not an intended part of nursing, our Maker wouldn't have provided it, so we have only to accept the gift and enjoy it.

Breastfeeding mothers sometimes look down with pity on bottlefeeding moms. They're not feeling superior; I think they're just puzzled as to why anyone would want to miss out on this beautiful experience. A good many years ago, women met with breastfeeding failure because of uninformed physicians and few practicing models to learn from. Today, besides living in a more enlightened society, we have books, films, helpful organizations, and even the sight of a nursing mother now and then to provide us with the knowledge we need. No one, however, will find it easy to pick up all this "know-how" at the last minute. A little planning and preparation is part of the picture, too.

A few guidelines to insure successful nursing are:

1. Somewhere around the sixth month of your pregnancy, locate a nursing league. La Leche League International, Inc., which offers support and encouragement to any woman who wants to nurse her baby, is the best known. Should you decide to join a similar group under a different name, be sure that it is medically endorsed. Of course, successful nursing doesn't depend upon your joining a special group of women, but when it comes to breastfeeding knowledge and technique, league members usually know more than the average physician.

2. Read, read, read. Women have surmounted all kinds of lactation problems with the help of books alone. Some outstanding books on breastfeeding are:

> *The Womanly Art of Breastfeeding*—La Leche League Int.
> *Nursing Your Baby*—Karen Pryor
> *The Tender Gift: Breastfeeding*—Dana Raphael
> *Abreast of the Times*—R. M. Applebaum, M.D.

3. Arrange for some kind of household help, not just for those trying postpartum days, but for the duration of your nursing experience. Weekly cleaning help may be out of the question, but a thorough "once a month" job can keep your house and your morale in good condition.

4. Begin streamlining your life. Meetings, volunteer work, and craft classes can wait. Some mothers even put aside gardening, sewing, and extensive cooking. You'll find that your body will set the limits, so when you're tired—rest.

5. Understand and be prepared for the emotions and special problems of a nursing mother. Preoccupation with baby, and a decreased sex drive are two common complaints, but there are others equally as frustrating. Accept these changes with the knowledge that things will return to normal when you wean the baby.

6. Learn to enjoy nursing from the beginning of motherhood. Perhaps you can make it a habit to stop whatever you're doing at least twice a day and sit down with a cup of tea while baby nurses. This is a lovely chance to relax, particularly if you have other small children.

Breastfeeding is a wonderful way to become acquainted with your child, but remember that this is only the beginning. For the love that you are now so carefully nurturing at the breast must continue to be the binding thread between the two of you forever and ever.

Outings— going out with baby

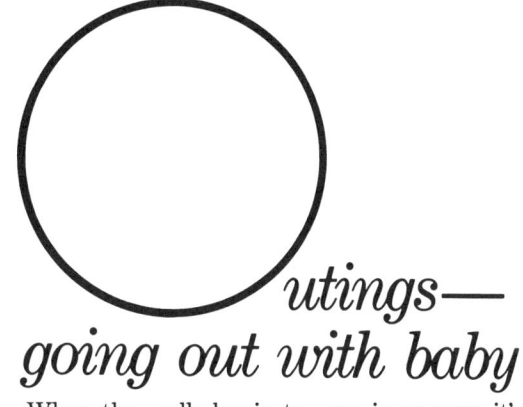

When the walls begin to cave in on you, it's time for a mother and child outing. Strangely enough, too much of the same routine can be as trying for the baby as it is on you. Why not pack your tote bag and take off on any one of these interesting jaunts?

Try:
- a trip to the zoo
- riding a bus
- eating outside on the patio
- a visit to the duck pond
- a spin through an art museum
- browsing through a flea market
- walking through the botanical gardens
- collecting rocks in a dry stream bed
- going to an ice cream parlor
- feasting on watermelon at the park
- visiting a state park

strolling through a shopping mall
visiting a pet store
backpacking
stargazing on a summer night
picnicking at the neighborhood playground
a sunrise bike ride

Things may not always come off as planned on your first few outings. The secret to successful adventures is being prepared for everything—even the worst. But the more you take baby out, the more adept you'll become at the game; and who knows, you just might come out as a winner every once in a while.

If we live in the Spirit, let us also walk in the spirit (Galatians 5:25).

Overweight— easy does it

Nature never intended for pregnancy to result in obesity. If you don't believe it, take a look at the sleek lines of a mother horse—or any animal for that matter. Somehow they come through the rigors of motherhood looking better than ever, while we humans seem to have adopted the slogan, "baby or body—you can't have both."

Probably the best way to insure yourself against excessive weight gain after pregnancy is to stay within the recommended weight boundary set by your doctor *during* pregnancy. I'd love to get hold of whoever started the rumor that a pregnant woman should eat for two. Nothing could be farther from the truth, and if you do eat twice as much of everything during pregnancy, you'll find yourself sadly overweight at the end of nine months. However, women who work hard to establish sensible eating habits during this time are likely to eat wisely for the rest of their lives.

Curbing an expectant mom's appetite isn't the easiest task, though, and you may have to work overtime just to stay one step ahead. Keep peeled cucumber and carrot sticks in the refrigerator, place a bowl of fresh fruit on the coffee table for late night television snacks, and stock up on a wide variety of vegetable and fruit juices. Learn to estimate the caloric value of foods and how to use these calories most effectively. For instance, a banana spread with a tablespoon of peanut butter is about 200 calories, just a little less than a chocolate bar—but much more filling and nutritious. And, a tomato slice on your melted cheese sandwich adds only token calories, but makes that sandwich seem like more of a meal.

Your six-week checkup will probably find you back to your prepregnancy weight, plus five or six pounds. A nursing mother will lose these extra pounds during the first few months of mothering, but if you are bottlefeeding or weaning a baby and still on the hefty side, now's the time to get that weight off.

Diets are almost fun nowadays, and the library will turn up a wide assortment of reducing ideas, from supervised fasts, to "all you can eat" vegetarian fare. Select one and then check with your doctor for medical clearance. My favorite reducing diet is the simple 1,000-calorie-a-day diet, because you can budget calories to include snacks and weekend eating. It's not a bad idea for all of us to count calories at least once in a while. Overweight doesn't just happen suddenly. It creeps up slowly but surely over a period of months—maybe years when we take in more food than our body can use.

If, for instance, you began the new ritual of a milkshake before bed each night and failed to add sufficient exercise to your agenda, it would eventually show up as uninvited weight. This type of weight gain can be a particularly bad problem among career women turned housewives. (Mopping the kitchen floor may have felt like hard work, but would you believe that you burned only 5.3 calories per minute?)

To find out how many calories you may eat each day in order to maintain your present weight, multiply that weight by 15.

_____ *(your present weight) x 15 = number of calories necessary to maintain your weight.*

You'll more than likely discover that you enjoy a normal, but moderate diet. You can, however, regulate your diet with exercise.

A sensible amount of exercise won't increase your appetite as many people think, but it may allow you to indulge in a dessert or snack that you'd otherwise be forced to forego. Walking is one of the best exercises that a mother can take up, for it's pleasantly relaxing, requires no partner, and involves no high fees. After the initial investment, biking claims many of these same advantages. Try to stay away from fancy spas which you probably wouldn't use enough anyway, and sports that call for only spurts of energy flow. Tennis, for example, is terrific if you can really play. But if you spend a lot of time standing, you'd best not count it as serious exercise.

Changes in your day-to-day life will also demand changes in your eating habits. Some women find that when the baby begins to walk they have to cut down on calories a bit, while others claim that the antics of a toddler enable them to eat far more. The important thing is to simply eat a well-balanced, nourishing diet. When you do, you'll discover that you eat only when you're hungry, crave fewer sweets, and know when to stop. And anyone who's in on these secrets should surely be slim for life.

Following is a five-day starter for your 1,000-calorie diet. With the help of a calorie counter, you can plan your diet each week as you make your family's grocery list.

DAY 1

		calories
Breakfast	1 fresh peach	50
	1 egg (boiled)	80
	1 slice toast	65
	1 tsp. butter	25
	coffee or tea, no sugar or cream	
Lunch	1 cup vegetable soup	80
	¼ cup cottage cheese	50
	lettuce	5
	1 slice whole-wheat bread	65
	1 apple	45
	1 6 oz. glass skim milk	60
Dinner	1 cup beef broth	25
	1 broiled lamp chop, thick fat removed	200
	1 small baked potato	80
	½ cup boiled carrots	25
	lettuce and tomato salad	25
	½ cantaloupe	50
	1 8 oz. glass skim milk	85

DAY 2

Breakfast	½ cup orange juice	50
	1 cup puffed rice	50
	1 6 oz. glass skim milk	60
	1 slice bacon	50
	coffee or tea, no sugar or cream	

Lunch	1 hamburger steak			1 tsp. sugar	15
	(lean ¼ lb.)	175		coffee or tea,	
	1 fresh tomato	25		no sugar or cream	
	1 cup beef broth	25			
	½ cantaloupe	50	*Lunch*	1 cup chicken soup	75
	1 6 oz. glass skim milk	60		1 slice melba toast	40
				1 tsp. butter	25
Dinner	1 cup tomato soup	100		lettuce and tomato salad	25
	1 breast of chicken			2/3 cup fresh cherries	45
	(roasted or boiled)	160		1 6 oz. glass skim milk	60
	½ cup spinach	20	*Dinner*	1 cup tomato juice	50
	cabbage salad	20		Baked ham (¼ lb.)	200
	1 slice whole-wheat bread	65		½ cup spinach	20
	1 cup custard	110		½ cup peas	60
	coffee or tea,			cabbage and carrot salad	40
	no sugar or cream			baked apple, laced with	
				diet soda	50
				1 8 oz. glass skim milk	85

DAY 3

Breakfast	½ cantaloupe	50
	1 egg (boiled)	80
	1 piece of toast	65
	1 tsp. butter	25
	coffee or tea,	
	no sugar or cream	
Lunch	5 breaded fish sticks	200
	¼ cup cottage cheese	50
	lettuce salad	5
	1 slice whole-wheat bread	65
	coffee or tea,	
	no sugar or cream	
Dinner	1 cup onion soup	100
	¼ lb. broiled salmon	200
	1 slice melba toast	40
	cauliflower salad	15
	1 fresh peach	45
	1 8 oz. glass skim milk	85

DAY 5

Breakfast	1 orange	50
	1 egg (boiled)	80
	1 piece of toast	65
	1 tsp. butter	25
	coffee or tea,	
	no sugar or cream	
Lunch	2 scrambled eggs	160
	fried with ½ tsp. butter	12.5
	1 tomato	25
	1 slice whole-wheat bread	65
	½ tsp. butter	12.5
	1 6 oz. glass skim milk	60
Dinner	Meatless vegetable soup	80
	Roast veal (¼ lb.)	200
	6 stalks asparagus	25
	1 small potato	80
	1 broiled potato	80
	1 broiled tomato	25
	1 cup fresh strawberries	50
	coffee or tea,	
	no sugar or cream	

DAY 4

Breakfast	1 cup fresh strawberries	50
	1 cup Special K cereal	60
	1 6 oz. glass skim milk	60

Pacifiers— the problem of "pacy"

For a while, it looked as if our youngest brother, Butch, might go off to the first grade with a pacifier dangling from his mouth. But despite the shocked glances he got from our neighbors and friends, Mother remained blasé. Butch was her fifth baby—her last child, and she, herself, was older, wiser, and more confident than ever before. "So what?" was her answer to sharp reprimands. And nobody, regardless of his stand on pacifiers, could help but admire Mother's spirit.

Pacifiers baffle many parents. If you're dead set against them, rest assured that someone will always be trying to convince you of their value. And if you've decided you kind of like the idea of a pacifier, people will flood you with criticism. Since you can't win, stop trying, and just let baby decide the issue for himself.

There are a lot of reasons for using the pacifier; most of them with your infant's best interest in mind. Colic or irritableness is one such example. When you've rocked, walked, fed, and goodness knows what else to quiet a crying baby, try the pacifier. If it works, perhaps baby's comfort is more important than any prejudices you might hold against the "pacy." Besides, a baby who does use the pacifier to get over bouts of fretfulness will usually outgrow his desire for it as he outgrows the colic (around three or four months).

A pacifier is also helpful in satisfying a baby's need for extra sucking. If your infant seems continuously hungry but spits up profusely after meals, he may simply be overeating to meet his sucking needs. Check with your physician to rule out illness, and then offer the pacifier; it may be just what baby's been looking for. This is a good trick for a nursing mother with sore nipples, too. When both breasts have been emptied, allow baby to finish his sucking on a pacifier until your nipples are in better condition.

Many experts tell us that a pacifier is less likely to push teeth out than the thumb. This could be because babies tend to give up the pacifier earlier than the thumb. But for those toddlers who seem reluctant to give up the good life, there are special pacifiers guaranteed not to cause overbite. And not nearly as scientific, but oh, so true, a pacifier is downright handy for comforting a hungry baby when bottle- or breastfeeding is impossible.

So, you see, there are some pretty good reasons for considering the use of a pacifier. But watch out, there are just as many reasons why you shouldn't. One of the most common complaints against the pacifier is that it so often becomes a mother substitute. When Mom discovers how easy it is to quiet baby with a rubber binky, she soon finds herself pushing the pacifier into his mouth instead of picking him up. And some women become so dependent on the pacifier that baby can scarcely whimper without having his mouth stuffed. Such abuse is entirely the fault of Mom, for when baby cries, what he really wants is *you* and what you as a mother have to offer—whether it's feeding or a warm hug.

The nursing mother should be particularly careful not to use the pacifier too much. It can sometimes satisfy a baby's sucking needs so well that he fails to nurse long enough at the breast, and a decrease in Mom's milk supply results.

Another problem with the pacifier is that it sometimes demands more work on your part than it's worth. Any time you find yourself getting up throughout the night to replace a crying baby's pacifier, you're losing valuable rest time. You might want to take the pacifier away and pat baby on his back when he wakes; it shouldn't be long before he'll sleep more peacefully. And probably the worst fear involved with the pacifier is that baby will become so attached to it, he simply won't give it up. This is when you're suddenly self-conscious about baby's funny looks with a pacifier in his mouth and those future teeth that everyone predicts will be malformed.

But what will you do if the pacifier is the answer for baby? First, do make sure that baby's pacifier is one of the special orthodontic creations. Second, watch for your cue. When a three-month-old starts spitting the pacifier out, it's time for Mom to put it away. Third, relax. Is a pacifier really so different from another child's security blanket? (We think nothing of a two-year-old carrying around an old blanket.) Of course, if your older baby is still addicted to his pacifier, you can expect a certain amount of criticism. Take it good-naturedly and continue to allow baby to set the pace just as you would with potty training or weaning. Some mothers gradually ease the pacifier out of the picture by hiding it when baby's not showing much interest. Others claim success by cutting tiny pieces off the pacifier each week until the remaining stub is so useless that baby willingly throws it away. (But be aware that a crumbly pacifier could cause choking.)

So, there you have it, the pros and cons of a pacifier. It's not nearly as serious a problem as new mothers think, and it's certainly not worth the energy you'll waste in worrying about it.

Let heaven fill your thoughts; don't spend your time worrying about things down here (Colossians 3:2, TLB).

Prayer— in praise of prayer

My meditation of him shall be sweet; I will be glad in the Lord (Psalm 104:34).

Shortly after my daughter's birth, a friend asked me to pray for her critically ill mother, and although I quickly agreed to, I was secretly hesitant. You see, there was no longer a regular prayer time in my life. Somehow, I had come to believe that in the world of colic and diapers, there was no time to be wasted on prayer.

Christian women are not immune to fatigue or busyness. Having a new baby leaves most women coping with a demanding schedule, neglected family members, and our own low spirits. And like all women, we take the responsibility of feeding and checking on baby so seriously that there is little time left over for our own needs. But unlike other women, we as Christian mothers have one additional responsibility—teaching our children a faith that will last them a lifetime. This means that even as infants, they must see us turn to the Lord each day for little things and simple conversations before we can expect them to rely upon God for solutions to major problems.

Prayer, however, isn't merely a teaching tool. It's a real gift to Mom. It puts those everyday crises into proper perspective, fills our heart with a tolerance for those things we can't change, gives us patience for conditions that will subside in time, and provides solutions to even the most stubborn obstacles. Too tired to pray? After deep prayer, we often feel so completely rested that one wonders if this in itself isn't a bonus that God intends for those who take time for him. At any rate, the inner strength that we obtain from prayer is something that no mother should deny herself.

But as one mother to another, I know the difficulty of praying during baby's naptime. Perhaps you're nursing and need the nap yourself, or maybe this is a special time between you and your other children. A wise friend helped me solve the dilemma. "Find hidden prayer time in your day," she said. And it does work.

WHEN TO FIND TIME

Convinced that you've no extra time? Take another look.

The 2:00 A.M. feeding. Some babies insist on that predawn snack well into the first year.

Instead of begrudging this nocturnal task, be happy that you have such a quiet time to spend in meditation without interference from siblings or even the ring of a telephone. Fix yourself a snack, draw the drapes just enough to glimpse the stars, and open your heart to God while baby satisfies his hunger.

The afternoon walk. A daily walk is a lovely habit to start, for it keeps you trim and gives baby a healthy glow to his cheeks. Besides that, it's a good time to talk silently to God. As you look at autumn leaves or summer lawns, you'll find it easy to share your thoughts with the Lord.

The midmorning snack. If your body groans at the mention of an in-between meal treat, try saving your own breakfast until everyone else has eaten and settled down to a morning activity. Sitting down to a cup of tea and a slice of toast is a natural during prayer and Scripture reading.

Cleaning time. It's never pleasant to spend spare time in cleaning, but occasionally we mothers must. That's when it's time to put an album of sacred music on the stereo. Turn the volume up to be heard throughout the house, and sing praises to the Lord.

When prayer doesn't come easily. All of us can remember being so depressed, at times, that prayer was the last thing on our mind. When this happens to you, sit down and begin thanking the Lord for all of the obvious good things in your life, such as shelter and clothing. Thanking God for his gifts usually breaks the ice for deeper communication, but even if it doesn't, you've still talked to God, and that's important because every day that we put prayer off makes it that much easier to slip from the habit.

Certainly the list of found prayer time doesn't have to end here. But your own private routine will be full of moments unheard of in another woman's life, so the question of when to pray should really be left up to you. One thing is for sure—the more time you find for prayer, the more you'll agree with me that prayer time is never wasted time.

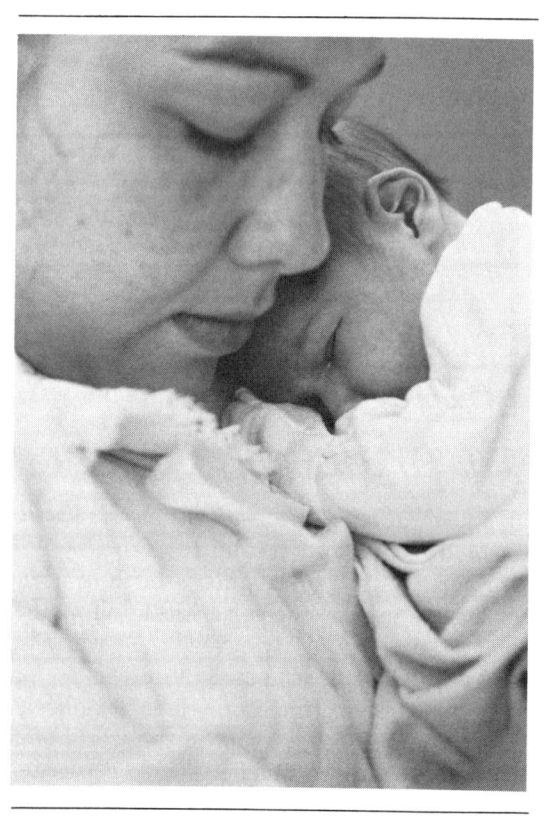

Quality of mothering—time: quality or quantity?

As a working mother, Susan's day begins early and ends late. Up at five to feed six-month-old Amy, she cannot even think of relaxing until well after midnight when an exhausting round of chores are completed. Susan is tired. And yet, her work prospers, her marriage thrives, and her mothering is blossoming into what she feels it should be. "I don't really care who feeds and diapers my baby," she says. "Isn't it more important to spend one good hour with my daughter every day?"

Susan's friend Janice is a full-fledged housewife and mother. She is not, however, passing her time in idle pursuit. What with all her household duties and her new community involvement, Janice is constantly on the go, and tucked under one arm is nine-month-old

Peter. "I'm not concerned with the fact that I rarely devote time exclusively to Peter. He's with me twenty-four hours a day, and isn't just being with me what's important?" she asked.

So there you have it—two very different women, each asking the same question. Which is more important, the quantity of time spent with a child or the quality of this time? I wonder where we got the idea it had to be one or the other. For it seems to me that quality mothering could be offered in as large or as small doses as we wanted. To get a better picture of how these things are related, perhaps you'd like to do the following exercise.

Make a list of all the things you have to do for your child and another list of all the things you would like to do for him. Your list might look something like this:

Things I have to do for my child:
    feed
    bathe
    diaper
    care for when ill
    provide clothing, toys, proper medical care

Things I'd like to do for my child:
    provide him with a comfortable atmosphere
    give him good memories
    give him the ability to handle stress
    give him the ability to make decisions
    give him a sense of honesty and sincerity
    give him love and the ability to love back

Would it surprise you to learn that the wonderful gifts in the second list quite often come about as an end result of those mundane chores in the first list? But it's true, for while you're performing the functional duties of motherhood, baby is being immersed in you, the person. He's taking in your smile, your voice, your scent, your very happiness or unhappiness. And although he's got a long way to go, he's slowly grasping your values and your outlook on life. So, put quality into the everyday business of living; it's more important than we sometimes realize. You can:

1. Make baby's bath more than a cleanliness routine. Purchase a book on infant swimming and help him become acquainted with the water.

2. Utilize your backpack for household chores. Being a real part of your world leaves a little one so satisfied. Maybe it's just that watching Mom knead bread is a hundred times more fun than a fancy mobile.

3. Talk to your baby as you feed, diaper, and tend to his needs.

4. Stop in the middle of your housework to pat a little head.

5. Encourage the use of new skills such as grasping, standing, and pulling up whenever the baby is in your lap.

6. Make sure that the baby is always placed in as interesting surroundings as possible. For instance, it may be easier to set up the playpen on the patio, but doesn't the shade of a tree offer a great deal more asthetically?

7. Provide colorful picture books and the best of music.

Of course, there are indeed times when quality mothering demands huge hunks of time, and even the most civic-minded mother may find that both she and the baby benefit greatly from an entire day at home once in awhile. "Oh, but I would be so bored with all that time on my hands," explained one woman. In this world of go, go, go, she speaks for many of us, doesn't she? But learn to appreciate the gift of free time; and sink into the luxury of enjoying your baby.

You might spend this time taking baby on an outing for his sake instead of yours. A walk through the park should be an opportunity for baby to look at flowers and listen to birds—not a gossip hour for you and other moms.

If several children or unusually large household obligations leave you with little time

Quiet Time— Hi, God

Those that seek me early shall find me (Proverbs 8:17b).

If you fail to teach your child anything else, don't neglect the area of prayer. For knowing how to talk with the Lord is one of the most valuable gifts that can be handed down to a youngster.

I can't remember when I first learned to pray; growing up as a minister's daughter, I knew God was always a part of our family. We prayed about everything from life-threatening situations to simple daily concerns like Friday night dates, and God always came through; we knew he would. People can learn to pray at any age, but those of us who have had the advantage of having prayed throughout life feel that the earlier a person learns to pray, the better off he is.

Probably the first prayer your child ever heard was a tearful, and somewhat emotional, prayer of thanksgiving for his safe delivery. But even if you chose to keep those thoughts between just you and God, the weeks ahead will provide ample opportunity for taking your little one to the Lord in prayer.

With my daughter, it was colic. Morning and night I took Heather into my arms and asked God to ease her discomfort. Most of the time it seemed as if he wasn't going to hear my prayers, for Heather's crying dragged on and on. But as Heather grew strong and healthy and more beautiful than my wildest dreams, I was comforted with the knowledge that God *did* care. Who knows? Perhaps God realized that I needed the added incentive of "trouble" to remember the importance of praying with my child. (Prayer does come easier when we're in need of something.) But you don't have to hunt for problems in order to build a strong mother-child prayer life. It all boils down to making the time.

Many adults think that the only suitable prayer for a child is the memorized prayer. And while there's nothing wrong with teaching these prayers to your child for a little variation, don't overlook the fact that being able to talk to God from your heart is really much more useful. And this is what it's all about. You're

---

to devote to an individual child, perhaps you could hire a preteen to help you with the other children while you tend to the one with the most need. One smart mother made arrangements with her church's mother's-day-out program for her children to take turns attending. This way each of her two children had one day every other week when Mom was all his.

There are as many different ways to add quality to your mothering as there are mothers. And the older your child becomes the more avenues you'll have to explore. For now, it's probably safe to say that as long as you're smiling, kissing, touching, and complimenting that baby as often as you can—you're on the right track. Your main goal as a high quality mother is to let your child know that he has added joy and happiness to your life. (And by the way, who can do that in one hour each day?)

Thank you, God for loving us. Amen.

Dear Lord, thank you for Daddy, and help him to have a good day. Amen.

Dear Heavenly Father, we enjoyed the sun today. Please give us another pretty day tomorrow. Amen.

---

trying to teach your child to use prayer as a tool for living so that someday he can move his own mountains. This kind of communication with God doesn't happen overnight and can rarely be accomplished with the occasional emergency prayers that we're all so guilty of succumbing to. It takes hours of practice and a great deal of discipline because prayer is an art that has to be learned.

Perhaps the easiest way to teach a child how to pray is to show him by example—pray for your baby in his presence. Blessings may already be a mealtime institution at your house, and that's good; but make sure that this isn't the only form of prayer that he hears. You can move the rocker to a secluded corner or sit out under the trees for a private encounter with the Lord now and then. During this time ask God to bless you as a mother and to help your child grow strong and healthy.

As baby gets older, you'll want to talk about things that pertain to his life. Thank God for a happy outing; or after a particularly trying day, ask him to give you both a better tomorrow. Bedtime prayers are especially adaptable to these simple conversations with God. A few examples of spontaneous prayers for your infant are above. Use them only as a guide, though. God wants to hear your thoughts —in your own words.

Sometimes a mother starts off with good intentions of praying with her infant, but as soon as life becomes hectic, prayer is the first thing to go. This could be because we allow our prayer life to become boring, talking to God about the same old things in the same old way every day. (Would anything be interesting under these circumstances?) Why not add a little variety to that prayer time with baby? One day you may want to sing a prayer. This could be your very own prayer set to a homemade tune, or it might be five minutes of really praising the Lord through a favorite hymn. Listen carefully to the words as you sing and lift your heart toward God; singing is a wonderful way of communicating with the Lord. On other days you may choose to pray the Lord's Prayer or another beautiful prayer that you've memorized. And, of course, you'll not want to forget the blessing before meals. Remember to keep these short and to the point and everyone, including husbands, will cooperate more willingly.

And they brought young children to him, that he should touch them . . . And he took them up in his arms, put his hands upon them, and blessed them (Mark 10:13a, 16).

We may not be able to have our children blessed as these New Testament mothers did, but we can still take them to the Lord in prayer. And, believe me, the blessing that awaits you and your infant is far too special to pass up.

Reading— to the bookworm with love

I love to read. So much, in fact, that my greatest fear in having a baby was that there might not be enough time for reading. I did manage to squeeze reading in, though—usually at times then I should have been resting. One day while straightening the mountain of books that seemed to always stand beside the rocker, I was a bit surprised to uncover my Bible on the bottom of the stack. Here I had been so worried about catching up with the best-seller list and my favorite monthly magazines that Bible study had taken, not second, but last place.

Finding time for the Word of God is still not easy for me. But I've discovered that if I keep my Bible in a special spot—completely off limits to other books and periodicals—it's less likely to get overlooked. In our house this spot is the top drawer of an antique buffet. It may be a nightstand, a kitchen cabinet, or an empty magazine rack at your house, but just make sure that the spot you choose is one that you have daily contact with.

Above all, enjoy reading your Bible. Never, never, should it be a chore. Change the pace every once in awhile by straying from organized Scripture lessons to explore on your own. With the help of a concordance, you can find various accounts of families, friends, celebrations, and much more. To get you started, here are some interesting stories of biblical mothers.

Read about:
- *Sarah's blessing*—Genesis 21:1-8
- *Rebekah's twins*—Genesis 25:19-34; 27:1-40
- *The mother of Moses*—Exodus 2:1-10
- *Ruth's child*—Ruth 4
- *The mother of Samson*—Judges 13
- *Hannah's family*—1 Samuel 1—2:21
- *Motherly love*—1 Kings 3:16-27
- *A mother's miracle*—2 Kings 4:8-37
- *Elisabeth's baby*—Luke 1:5-80
- *The birth of Christ*—Luke 2
- *A mother's request*—Matthew 20:20-23
- *Mothers who loved Jesus*—Mark 10:13-16
- *Christ's compassion for a mother*—Luke 7:11-15

Romance— when three's a crowd

Dear Gloria,

I'm glad you sent that letter describing the frustrations of being a wife as well as a mother. I too can remember those early days of motherhood and the distance that began to grow between Olie and me. So, I know how difficult it can be to keep your marriage as it was before the baby arrived, and maybe I can help.

You know, it takes longer than six weeks after the birth of a baby for a marriage to return to normal. Those first few weeks are spent in celebration and recuperation, the next few in learning how to care for your baby, and somewhere between twelve and twenty-eight weeks are spent in simply trying to keep up with what seems like a never-ceasing list of baby demands.

It's no small wonder that our husbands become second-class citizens, practically overnight. I once told myself that since Olie could obviously feed, bathe, and entertain himself, I needn't feel guilty about spending so little time on him. After all, my job was to take care of a helpless infant who couldn't do these things for herself. But although it sounded like such a logical conclusion, things just weren't working out. Both of us hungered for the "old" life and the spouse we'd fallen in love with.

A good marriage is kind of like a strong sapling—it can certainly take a little bending without causing too much harm. And we usually put it to the test during family crises such as birth, death, and financial stress. But the trick is to know just how far your marriage will bend before snapping in two. No one can tell you when this will be—it depends entirely on the individuals and circumstances involved. It is, however, pretty safe to say that a woman who is tuned-in to life will recognize her husband's silent pleas for attention and the point at which things simply cannot go on as they are any longer.

Lately, you've been more of a mother than a wife, and it's not going to be easy to reconstruct your home life. You may discover that you don't even want to. "Let him make some of the effort," I used to complain. But this is one time that only you, the woman, can put that magical spark called romance back into your marriage.

When I got married my mother said, "Jayne, there's one bit of advice about marriage I'm going to pass on to you. Living together so closely, you'll soon discover that little things begin to annoy you, and it seems that it's the wife who does all the work. But when this happens to me, I always go back in my mind to when I first met your father. I thought he was the most wonderful man alive. And remembering him like that makes me realize that he's still the most wonderful man—only now I know he's human."

And so it is with most marriages, but particularly after the arrival of a new baby. Your husband may not be perfect; in fact, the pressure of parenthood may have uncovered a number of faults previously unknown to you. But he's still that wonderful man you married, and if you'll give him the same love and tenderness that you gave so freely as a bride, he'll be the strong, dependable man whom you need so badly. Surely this reward is worth the sacrifice of making that first move toward romance. In a letter to Jewish Christians, Peter gives advice that all new parents would do well to heed.

Most important of all, continue to show deep love for each other, for love makes up for many of your faults (1 Peter 4:8, TLB).

When I was a new mother, I hung this verse over my kitchen sink as a reminder that love was more important than folded diapers and spotless floors. Then I sat down and developed my own love strategy which I'm sharing with you.

1. Of course, you're taking care of your appearance—dressing neatly, smelling good, and exercising faithfully. Now, choose a usually ordinary night like Monday and greet your husband at the door in a hostess gown complete with earrings and necklace. Not only will you enjoy looking special, but it'll warm your husband's heart to know that he's still important enough to merit your best dress.

2. Prepare a midnight feast to be eaten off a tray in your bedroom. For a man-pleasing snack, serve large baked potatoes with a variety of condiments—real butter, sour cream and chives, shredded cheddar cheese, bacon chips, and salt and pepper.

3. Go out—just the two of you for a few hours. Even a nursing mother can leave her little one for two hours. A few places to spend two hours are: a movie theater, a restaurant, a friend's house, a quiet country road. Try not to do exhausting things such as walking through botanical gardens or playing tennis.

4. On your absolute worst day, set a candle on the table and *voila!*—a candlelight dinner. Did you ever know a woman who could bring up the broken washing machine and the baby's diaper rash over a flickering candle and soft music?

5. Surprise your husband with a love box full of paper clips and rubber bands. Directions: Paste magazine pictures of lovers, sunsets, children, etc., on a small cardboard box. Shellac for a shiny finish.

6. Turn your bedroom into a private retreat. One set of pretty sheets, a scented candle, and an FM radio do wonders for a romantic interlude.

7. Put Hubby first once in awhile. For instance, when the baby is crying for simple attention and you're in the middle of pouring your husband's coffee, let the baby cry until you've taken care of your man. Sounds like obvious advice, but I was amazed when my husband pointed out the number of times that I told him to "get his own coffee," while I tended to the baby.

8. Housewives tend to meet their husbands at the end of the day with a long list of "do's" and a demand for help with the baby. If you find yourself thinking of your husband as nursemaid relief, think twice. Remember, he's already put in his eight hours, and while it's true that as a mother you work 'round the clock, there are ways to make it easier on yourself. Accept the fact that the busiest time of day for you may be between five and seven P.M., and plan your daily activities accordingly. To assure yourself the energy you'll need to be a loving wife, take naps during the day and never use all of your strength on housekeeping.

9. Have a romantic picnic for two. All you need for a lover's picnic is a loaf of French bread, a block of cheese, olives, and a thermos of spice tea.

10. Praise your husband for his fathering skills, for his eagerness to help, and for his lovemaking. Everyone appreciates knowing his worth.

So there you have it—how Olie and I got it all together again. If you can just follow through on these few suggestions, you probably won't have to think of any on your own, because one of the nicest things about romance is that with just a tiny bit of encouragement, a small spark can grow into a huge fire.

I'm expecting to hear some wonderful results.

*Love,
Jayne*

Schedules— time out

For a long time it seemed that I could never keep up with my friend, Joan. No matter how hard I tried, my floors were never as shiny, my meals never as hearty, and my child never as well behaved as hers. It was quite by accident that I discovered her secret. We were having our apartment painted and Heather and I were spending the day with Joan in order to avoid the fumes.

As I watched my friend from morning till dark, I noticed that although she wasn't on a schedule in the strictest sense of the word, she led a very ordered and structured sort of life. There were certain things that she did at certain times. Nothing was put off because of unpleasantness and nothing was allowed to become all-consuming.

The possibilities that such a life style could

offer my own family excited me so that I could hardly wait to get home and reexamine my own time. And it was amazing what a difference just a little bit of organization made. Of course, being a lover of casualness, I couldn't bear to admit to being on a schedule, and in truth, I wasn't. I had simply devised a plan for making my day run in a more orderly fashion.

You, too, can organize your day without falling prey to a rigid hourly time schedule. Here are ten ways to help you get a head start in the race against time.

1. Decide what your priorities are. These are not always the things we want to do, but rather the things that we must do in order to be at peace with ourselves. For instance, you may enjoy watching television all day, but feel that attending to household duties is more important. Or you may appreciate a clean house, but feel that playing with baby is what it's all about. Priorities are a very individual matter, but they are the things you should strive to do each day before attempting the extras.

2. There will always be those things which we hate to do—but must. Try doing your most dreaded chore at that time of day when your energy is at a high. So what if this means leaving the dinner dishes overnight—is there any law against it?

3. Make a weekly list of the things you hope to accomplish. What fun you'll have in crossing items off!

4. Hire people to do the most strenuous jobs such as window cleaning and lawn mowing. Your hired help doesn't have to be professional or even adult; teenagers can be valuable friends to have.

5. Hire people to do those things that require an expert's touch. Sewing, hair coloring, and upholstery are just a few of these jobs.

6. Keep in touch with new products and time-saving ideas by subscribing to a good family-oriented magazine.

7. Reevaluate how you are presently spending your time. If you're in need of a few more hours, you may not be using baby's early morning and late night hours to your best advantage.

8. Make sure that the care of fancy appliances and beautiful furniture isn't draining you of energy.

9. Have simple daily goals. Giving yourself a manicure or sewing a button on Hubby's shirt can give you a great sense of accomplishment when you're caring for a little one.

10. Ask for God's guidelines in planning your activities. He alone can give you the strength, the calm, and the wisdom that you need to get through the day.

To help you evaluate your day, fill in the blanks below.

Things I must do: _____
_____
_____

Things I should do—but don't have to:
_____
_____
_____

Things I like to do: _____
_____
_____

Things I hate to do: _____
_____
_____

Now using the chart provided, divide each day of the week into three segments—morning, afternoon, and evening. Place those things which you must do in their most workable time slot. Next, find a time period for one thing you want to do. (Notice that we're not talking about hours; only a general time of day.) Last of all, check to make sure that you aren't tied down to dreary obligations that don't really matter. Because in addition to caring for your family, there should be time for rest, fun, and meditation in every day. But most important, when the day is over and you've done all that you could humanly manage, don't try to do more. Stand on what you've accomplished and be proud of it.

A mother's prayer:
Dear Lord,
*   As I start each day, help me to rearrange my priorities so that I am receptive to God's love and guidance, and am willing to place these things first. Amen.*

DAY	MORNING	AFTERNOON	EVENING
MONDAY			
TUESDAY			
WEDNESDAY			
THURSDAY			
FRIDAY			
WEEKEND			

Singing—homemaker's hymns

If the melody of a certain song has ever carried you back to your childhood, then you already know the impact that music can have upon our lives. Surely no other recreation can give us the same kind of enjoyment or fill our soul with the same feelings of inspiration.

Children need to be exposed to all forms of music, from classical to rock. And they need to take part in all kinds of musical adventures, from outdoor concerts to raucous family music nights.

Most of all, children need to sing and be sung

to. This is basic—the way most of us are first introduced to the joy of music. Without such a beginning, a child is likely to be labeled as unmusical, when the truth is, he was simply never given the opportunity to discover his potential.

I've had people ask me if a Christian mother should make a point of teaching her children sacred music, and I think I can safely say, "No, she doesn't have to." Praising the Lord through song just comes naturally to the Christian mother. We rock our infants to the tune of old-time gospel hymns, and we teach our toddlers the same action songs that we ourselves learned in Sunday school, without so much as realizing what we're doing. But when none of these come to mind, the book of Psalms is full of lovely songs. All you need add is a tune. Just think, here's your chance to compose, and with the most appreciative audience ever—your baby. So, praise the Lord in song, and sing to your baby as much as possible; the two go together so nicely.

Here are a few Scripture verses that are often used in simple praise songs.

Bless the Lord, O my soul: and all that is within me, bless his holy name
Psalm 103:1.

This Scripture can be arranged and rearranged into any number of songs. One popular combination is:

Bless the Lord
Oh my soul
Bless the Lord
Bless his holy name.

Don't forget, you're making up the tune. But if you're about to back out, I'll confess that I've often arranged the Psalms to fit a particular "known" tune.

Now here's a verse that lends itself to fun and action.

O clap your hands, all ye people; shout unto God with the voice of triumph
Psalm 47:1.

Introduce this song to your nine-month-old baby and watch him clap with gladness.

Oh clap your hands (clap two times)
Oh clap your hands (clap two times)
All ye people, clap your hands.

Shout unto God (clap two times)
Shout unto God (clap two times)
All ye people, shout unto God (shout hallelujah).

Unto thee, O Lord, do I lift up my soul
Psalm 25:1

This single sentence makes a beautiful song of repetition, and a soothing lullabye besides.

Show me thy ways, O Lord; teach me thy paths. Lead me in thy truth, and teach me: for thou art the God of my salvation; on thee do I wait all the day Psalm 25:4, 5.

Like so many of the Psalms, these verses adapt nicely into simple songs. One example that is especially easy for a child to sing is:

Show me, Lord
Teach me, Lord
Lead me in thy truth.

Most of the Psalms are so rhythmic that we can sing them just as they are. Psalm 96:1, 2 is one of these.

O sing unto the Lord a new song: sing unto the Lord, all the earth. Sing unto the Lord, bless his name; show forth his salvation from day to day.

Of course, let me remind you that these are only one woman's favorite Psalms. Why not spend a few moments finding your own songs of praise. You'll enjoy singing them as much as baby enjoys hearing them. And before you know it, you'll have actually memorized some of the Bible's most beautiful passages.

Remember what Christ taught and let his words enrich your lives and make you wise; teach them to each other and sing them out in psalms and hymns and spiritual songs, singing to the Lord with thankful hearts (Colossians 3:16, TLB)

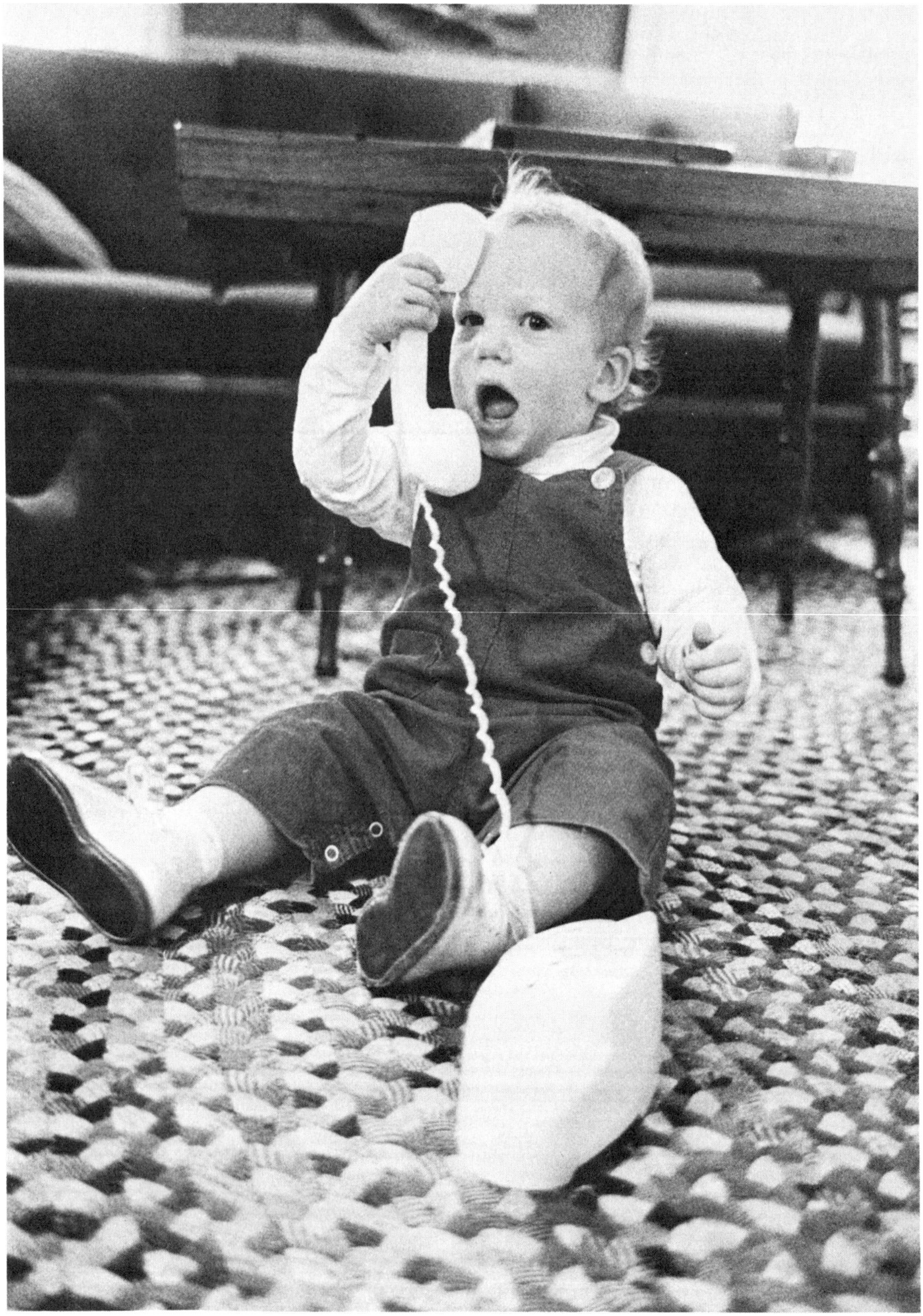

Toys—
toy talk

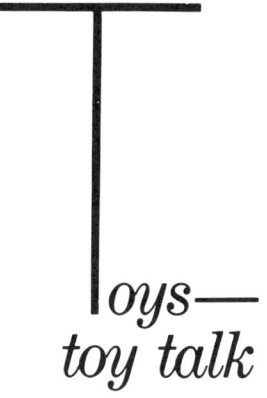

It was a familiar scene—a mother and dad giving last-minute instructions to the teenage baby-sitter—when suddenly they were confronted with, "But where are the children's toys?"

"Oh, they don't have many toys," the young mother quipped. Then, as if to make the situation admirable, she added, "We'd rather the children learn to use their imaginations."

A home without toys; how sad. Yet in these times, when "getting back to nature" is becoming a way of life, many young parents are guilty of shunning toys along with other plastic commodities. This is all fine and good to some extent—toys can be expensive. Besides, some are poorly made and many are downright dangerous (in spite of stricter safety requirements). But it's certainly a practice that shouldn't be overdone. Children need toys. Toys help them learn how to use their bodies and how to live in our world. And toys can add spice to our children's lives. When you look at it that way, a new toy every day isn't even too much.

Sound terribly unrealistic to your pocketbook? Not when you consider that you've already purchased those toys that will give your child the longest hours of pleasure. For they are the articles of everyday life; the things you cook with, dress in, or automatically throw away. After all, even a baby knows that taking part in life is what it's all about.

It's never too soon to start using your initiative as a parent. While there's no denying that a fancy store-bought mobile will entertain an infant grandly, a ball of aluminum foil suspended on a string across the crib bars will provide even greater fascination. Your baby will also be pleased with a magazine picture taped to one end of his crib, and in a few minutes you can replace the picture with a new one each day.

As soon as baby begins to reach for objects, you can begin raiding the house for suitable playthings that will sustain his interest well into his first year. Pots and pans are old standbys, but don't overlook other kitchen gadgets—jar lids, a stack of plastic drinking cups, cookie cutters, short-handled wooden spoons, a basting stick, an old coffee pot with the center stem removed, a clean sponge, and an empty plastic bottle make a fine start for your "home" toy collection. You can scavenge for more toys in the rest of the house. An old felt hat, a pair of Daddy's shoes, a stack of discarded magazines, Mommy's extra handbag, a box of dominoes, a set of "real" keys, cardboard boxes and tubes, and spools will be obvious choices, but there's no limit to the number of interesting surprises you can come up with.

Your only boundary is safety. Some objects may have sharp points, be painted with questionable paint, or be so small that they are easily swallowed and should never be given to a small child.

After you've discovered the joy hidden away in your closets and cabinets, you'll find that you do indeed purchase fewer but higher quality toys. That's not to say that you won't purchase small surprises for your baby now and then—of course you will. But even so, you'll save money, because when the measuring spoon set and the watering can are no longer needed for make-believe, they're yours for keeps.

Traveling— from here to there

We were loading the car for a three-day trip. As I handed Olie yet another suitcase, I glanced over at the mountain of baby equipment and wished for the simplicity of yesteryear.

"What I need is some travel advice from the world's greatest mothers," I thought aloud.

But you know what? I'll bet if we could question some of history's most famous mothers on the subject of travel, they'd all say the same thing. "Enjoy it—you've got it made."

Take Mary, the mother of Jesus, for instance. Every year Joseph took his family to Jerusalem for the Feast of the Passover. Like you and me, Mary must have been somewhat hesitant about holiday trips. The excitement of a vacation is too much to resist, but the work involved for Mom is another story. Mary didn't have to decide whether or not to take baby's swing, or calculate the number of disposable diapers she'd need, but she did have to expose her family to filth, disease, and makeshift accommodations all along the way.

And Jesus wasn't her only child, so there were probably very few trips on which Mary was not either pregnant or nursing an infant. Maybe she'd remind us that babies are really a lot easier to travel with than older children. One thing's for sure, if you ever reach the point in your globetrotting that you begin to feel inadequate, Mary would understand. Remember when she lost twelve-year-old Jesus?

Yes, times have changed, but mothers haven't. Traveling with baby is still not easy in spite of transportation marvels. A simple trip represents hours of careful thought. Here's how some of us manage.

PLANNING AHEAD

Now that baby's here, no more meandering holiday jaunts. You should know well in advance how you will travel and where you will be going. This not only enables you to make reservations for lodging that can equip you with a crib, it also determines what kind of preparations must be made for baby's food. Ah, the simplicity of breastfeeding. Mother's milk is always sanitary, always warm, and always there. But for a fairly reasonable price, even the bottlefeeding mother can claim convenience. Today's prepared formulas come in premeasured bottles that require no refrigeration, no preheating, and can be thrown away after use.

Of course, if you'll only be traveling for twenty-four hours or less, there's no need to go to this expense. You can prepare your formula at home and pack it in an ice chest or an insulated bag. Use your own bottles lined with disposable nurser bags for easy cleaning up. If baby insists upon warm milk, stop at a roadside cafe and ask the waitress to heat the bottle for you. Or if traveling by plane, a flight attendant will gladly help out.

Traveling for any extended length of time will involve taking an adequate supply of formula with you. Undoubtedly the prepared formula is the number-one choice, but when it's price is a little out of range, you can do just as well with powder or concentrated formula and a good supply of distilled water. The utensils that you'll have to use to prepare formula can be kept free of growing bacteria by simply washing them with soap and water as soon as you finish using them.

Things begin to get a little more complicated when baby starts to eat solids. This is when those commercial foods that you might shun at home are heaven sent. Select foods that are well liked and familiar. If baby must be fed from your plate, offer him nongreasy, hot foods. Avoid cold meats, fish, eggs, milk puddings, and cream-filled pastries, as these foods are among those most likely to cause illness. Carrying a thermos of distilled water and peeling your own fruit are two other safety measures you'll want to consider.

Some mothers wouldn't dream of going a city block without a snack pack. There's something comforting about nibbling, no matter what our age. Instead of giving baby candy sticks, round hard candy, and peanuts that might be easily choked on, try packing a generous portion of toasted whole-wheat bread slices. You'll find this treat much easier for baby to digest and much easier for you to clean up after. Your snack pack can also be thought of as a mini-survival kit, for on any trip that will carry you away from home, it should include a twenty-four-hour supply of emergency baby food.

PACKING

Even when you're packing tight for the rest of the family, baby needs two bags—a suitcase and a tote bag. I call the suitcase baby's overnight bag because this is usually the one I don't have access to until we're in our motel room. Into this bag go all the things I would normally need for a given time period at home—only twice as much of everything. Here's a simple list, which I hope will encourage you to write out your own before each trip.

- disposable diapers and box of baggies to seal soiled diapers in
- washcloths (the soft disposable dishtowels can be cut up to make dandy throw-away washcloths)
- towels
- lap pads (disposable lap pads can be made by cutting up inexpensive plastic tablecloths found in the paper goods department of any grocery)
- disposable bibs
- blankets
- knit gowns
- dress up clothes
- lotion, powder, cotton balls and swabs, soap, shampoo
- aspirin, thermometer
- dirty clothes bag (a pillow case will do)

The tote bag never leaves my side suring the entire trip. Some things to put in this bag are:

- disposable diapers and diaper wipes
- travel size lotion and powder
- premoistened disposable wash-ups
- a large plastic sack for soiled diapers
- a cup for the baby who can share Mom's beverage
- a bib
- snack pack
- surprise bag (a selection of interesting items for play)

This may sound like a lot to squeeze into a bag that you'll be carrying on your shoulder, but keep in mind that you need only pack small quantities of everything.

ON YOUR WAY

Regardless of how you plan to travel—plane, train, boat, or car, make arrangements for baby's comfort. For the very long flights, airlines will often provide a bassinet if asked ahead of time. At any rate, try to sit in the front of the plane's cabin, as there really is a bit more room in this area. Car travelers can set up a car bed in the back seat for the tiny baby, while an older baby will be both happier and safer in a car seat. Then later, when baby is sleepy, a few pillows and his favorite blanket will make your lap a snug bed. Clothing should also be comfortable. Dress baby simply, and protect your own garment with a smock.

SAFETY RULES FOR CAR TRAVEL

1. Keep baby in the car seat for as long as possible.
2. Watch little fingers when shutting doors.
3. Keep windows closed; doors locked.
4. Avoid sudden stops.
5. Don't hand baby across from front to back of car or vice versa.
6. When baby needs tending, pull over and stop the car.
7. Open the door on the curb side.
8. Don't offer baby sharp toys or food that can be easily choked on.
9. Don't worry about making good time. Stop often for coffee breaks.
10. Give yourself a rest—let Dad watch baby while you drive.

Travel gives us a sense of freedom, broadens our outlook on life, and provides us a break in the everyday business of living. Most of all, traveling makes home look good. What mother doesn't need that kind of a lift once in awhile?

Unhappiness—today is a happy day

One evening as we were eating in a hamburger restaurant, I happened to notice another young family seated to our side. The baby was gurgling contentedly, the father was eating with zest, and the mother sat staring into space as if terribly unhappy. Feeling a bit guilty to be intruding upon her privacy, I quickly turned away. But curiosity won the battle, and I stole just one last glance.

Goodness, that was myself! I had been looking at my own reflection in the plate-glass window. And yes, I was unhappy at the moment. Some small thing that had happened to me during the day had left me feeling as if I were the poorest, the loneliest, and the most overworked mother in the world.

Being unhappy is just as much a sin as hating or stealing. It's kind of like saying this great, big, wonderful world created by God isn't good enough. And yet, I suppose this is one shortcoming we can all claim. God not only knows this side of our nature, he wants to help us through these times—he wants us to be happy. Evidence of this love is found over and over again in the Bible's comforting words. My own father once said, "The Bible isn't a rule book. The Bible simply holds secrets for living."

How true. So if you are unhappy or depressed, search for these secrets until you, too, can smile again. Better yet, why not look for them ahead of time and keep them handy for those blue days. Here are a few of the usual causes for a mother's unhappiness and Scripture verses which are sure to help. Share them with a friend.

THE UNPLEASANT BIRTH EXPERIENCE

I remember reading a magazine article that claimed having a baby was no longer enough—now you have to do it better than anyone else. Sound familiar? Today there are many parents who insist that unless your delivery was unmedicated, the lights dimmed, and your camera constantly in action, you've never really experienced birth. These people can be so convincing that a lot of mothers leave the hospital with a feeling of defeat that takes months or even years to overcome.

It's all kind of silly. I know, because when my own daughter was delivered by an operative rather than a Lamaze birth, I felt I had been robbed of life's greatest mystery. But as Heather grew and developed in all ways, I learned that motherhood was much more than giving birth. And you will too.

Whatever happens, dear friends, be glad in the Lord (Philippians 3:1a, TLB).

COPING

After the initial excitement of having a baby wears off, life returns to normal for everyone but you. Hubby goes back to work, Grandma returns to her own family, and visiting friends are busy with everyday living. Somehow, you feel that you, too, should get hold of yourself and begin managing things better. But the baby still keeps you up most of the night, your days are still spent folding and changing diapers, and your muscles are still weary from the experience of birth itself.

Be patient. You're probably suffering from a touch of baby blues. Rest assured that all will be well within a week or two, and if it's not, your doctor can prescribe medication that will help. It might be, however, that you simply expected motherhood to be different than it has turned out to be.

The disappointment of a crying baby and a hectic life style is enough to make anyone unhappy. Turn this matter over to God. He has given you the job of mothering because he wants you there, and he will help you adjust and be happy in your new role.

For the battle is not yours, but God's (2 Chronicles 20:15b, TLB).

TOO MUCH WORK

It may be that your first real problem as a mother is work, or perhaps I should say the abundance of it. There is a period in every new mother's life when it seems that there'll never again be a spare minute just for sitting, and the very thought is enough to get you down. Cheer up, things do get better as baby grows older. In the meantime, let this verse be your motto.

The joy of the Lord is your strength (Nehemiah 8:10b, TLB).

MARITAL ADJUSTMENT

So the baby has come between you and your husband. Stay calm—it happens to most of us. Learning to love two people is not easy when you're used to centering your life on just one person. And even experienced moms find it difficult to make time for Hubby when other demands seem more pressing. Reread the chapter on romance, then pray and believe. God realizes how important a strong marriage is to you *and* your baby, and he'll hear your prayer.

> *What things soever ye desire, when ye pray, believe that ye receive them, and ye shall have them* (Mark 11:24).

FINANCIAL STRAIN

It's a rare mom, indeed, who isn't, at least once in a while, unhappy with her family's financial status. Sure, it takes money to live, but I don't think any of us realize just how much until there's a baby to raise. Suddenly the doctor bills, clothing expenses, and grocery receipts become unsurmountable. Evenings out, disposable diapers, and household help can become as foreign sounding as the North Pole.

Sometimes these financial problems are short-lived, and sometimes they're not. So it behooves all of us to learn to be happy in spite of the lack of money. Take advantage of free entertainment such as parks, browse regularly through used furniture and clothing stores, sell any of your own "white elephants" at a flea market, and join a grocery co-op. In a day and age when such things are "in," there's no need to feel poor. Take stock of what you do have and all that can be done with it. Chances are, you'll be amazed at how good God has been to you as a family.

> *In every thing give thanks: for this is the will of God in Christ Jesus concerning you* (1 Thessalonians 5:18).

HOLDING A GRUDGE

As Christians we almost always recognize our sins and ask for forgiveness, but when it comes to forgiving someone else for a wrong done to us—well, that's different. Have you ever forgiven someone vocally and still hung on to a private grudge? I have. And nothing can create more unhappiness. You may not be able to forgive and forget; our memories are probably too well trained to forget anything unpleasant anyway. But you can ask God to help you deal with forgiving. When you do, you will more than likely discover that you are able to overlook the faults of the offender, and your peace is restored.

> *Be gentle and ready to forgive; never hold grudges. Remember, the Lord Jesus forgave you, so you must forgive others* (Colossians 3:13, TLB).

Unity of family— playing fair

During Olie's graduate school days our next-door neighbors became the proud parents of a baby boy. At the time, motherhood seemed as impossible to me as traveling to the moon for a holiday. "What's it like to have a baby in the family?" I asked. (Olie and I had been married only a short time and children were far away in our plans.)

"Well," the young mother answered, "before the baby, our love flowed back and forth between the two of us with the rhythm of a swing. Now our life is something like a triangle—it moves freely and unselfishly among the three of us, never stopping long enough to break the shape."

Although I thought her statement poetic, it wasn't until I had given birth to Heather that I realized how fitting it was. Paul illustrates this very triangle in Ephesians when he explains God's order for the Christian family. It is a pattern of love that is never broken, regardless of each person's responsibility to his family.

You wives must submit to your husbands' leadership in the same way you submit to the Lord. For a husband is in charge of his wife in the same way Christ is in charge of his body the church (Ephesians 5:22, 23, TLB).

But because submission alone is hardly enough to nurture love, Paul goes on to add:

And you husbands, show the same kind of love to your wives as Christ showed to the church when he died for her (Ephesians 5:25, TLB).

And then to further complete the triangle and to help solve the age-old problem of parent versus child, he gives even more advice:

Children, obey your parents; this is the right thing to do because God has placed them in authority over you (Ephesians 6:1, 2, TLB).

But again, obedience itself does little to encourage the flow of love, so Paul cautions:

And now a word to you parents. Don't keep on scolding and nagging your children, making them angry and resentful. Rather, bring them up with the loving discipline the Lord himself approves, with suggestions and godly advice (Ephesians 6:4, TLB).

Paul is speaking of a special kind of love, involving much give and take. He doesn't suggest that it is going to be easy. In fact, we will all fall short of the "ideal family" many times during our life. But the fact that we are a Christ-centered family is what gives us our strength, for he will lead the way through love.

God believes in the family. At no time has he ever condoned the destruction of a family through divorce, infidelity, or homosexuality. The family is one of man's most treasured gifts from God. For it is only by being a part of such a unit that we can understand the special happiness of just being around one another, the fierce loyalty among brothers and sisters, and those funny private jokes that add warmth and color to everyday life.

It's a good idea for expectant couples to discuss their parenting philosophies long before the baby arrives. If the two of you have been sharing a relaxed equal partnership, perhaps it's time to take stock of things. Ask yourself which is more important—riding with the times or placing Dad at the head of the family as Christ intended?

As a mother, it may be difficult for you to submit to your husband when it comes to child rearing, especially if you are on opposite poles of an issue. Our family went through such a crisis when Heather began exploring. I wondered if we were not a little too permissive, but her scientist father wanted her to feel and smell and listen to everything that captivated her interest.

Olie was the head of our family, and so Heather touched and touched to her heart's content. Somehow it all worked out, for we managed to reach a medium of understanding. Sure, Olie's word was law, but out of respect to me he saw to it that Heather's freedom was never at my expense. And that's what being a family is all about—working together for the best of everyone.

Mothers often find that strengthening family ties lies entirely in their hands. Not only is this task far from impossible, it can offer a lot of fun and challenge. Begin by instituting the custom of weekend family outings. (No baby-sitters for Saturday afternoons, please.)

Another experience that can enrich your family life is a time of daily devotionals with each other. Perhaps an evening prayer with Mother and Dad is all that the very young baby will enjoy, but the length of devotional time can grow as he does.

Some families like to "roughhouse" together. (Pillow fights and jumping on a bed can be surprisingly fun for even an old stick-in-the-mud like myself.) Just be sure that such activities stay within reasonable bounds. And despite the negative comments that we hear about television and children, this is a fairly good way to come together as a family. Selecting shows carefully and then watching the program as a group can be as pleasant as any elaborate outing.

As you build your family, remember your place, as the mother, in the unit. Be gentle and yet unyielding to the ways of the devil. Encourage each member of the family to respect other members. Never allow family members to speak unfavorably about each other. Teach even the youngest member of the family to understand the needs of other members.

Last of all, accept the responsibility and authority granted to you as a mother and use it wisely. For the love that God gave you and your husband is from this point on eternal and everlasting in the form of a triangle.

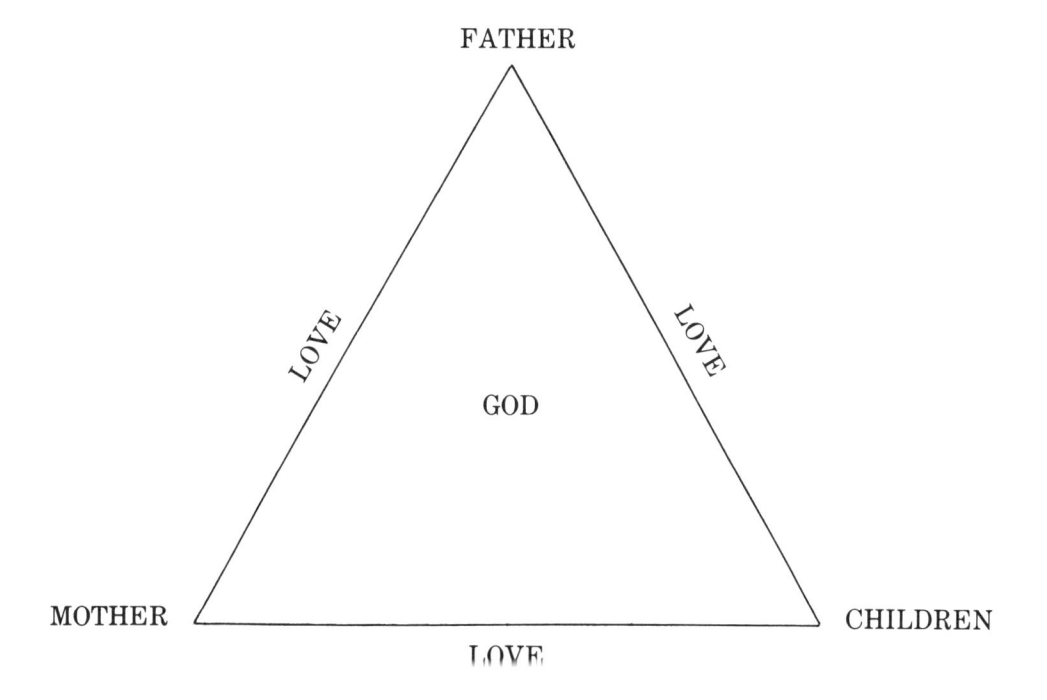

```
            FATHER
             /\
            /  \
       LOVE/    \LOVE
          /      \
         /  GOD   \
        /          \
       /            \
MOTHER /_____\ CHILDREN
            LOVE
```

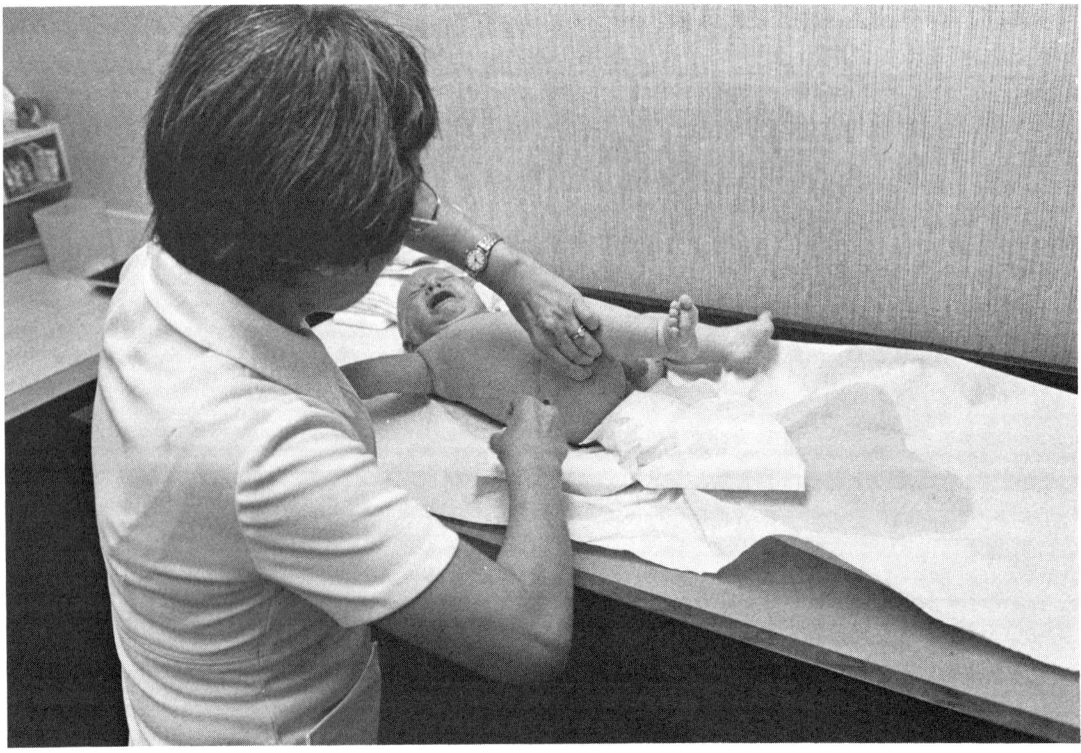

Vaccinations— keeping up with baby's health

Breastfeeding and a balanced diet can go a long way toward protecting your baby against illness, but they should never be thought of as substitutes for recommended immunizations. Today many parents, believing that diseases such as polio no longer pose a serious threat, are becoming quite lax about immunizing their children. Unfortunately, polio, diphtheria, whooping cough, tetanus, measles, and mumps are still very much alive and just as dangerous as ever. Should there ever come a time when these inoculations are not necessary, your physician will let you know. (The smallpox vaccination is one such example.) In the meantime, the Christian mother will want to do her part in protecting the health of her family.

Don't depend upon the doctor or nurse to keep you posted on which immunizations your child should have and when. If you ask, they will gladly supply you with a schedule and perhaps even a record card for keeping track of the dates on which the inoculations were given. Tape the schedule where you can keep your eye on it during baby's first year—then place it in your favorite child-care book for easy reference.

MEDICAL RECORD

Diphtheria _____
Whooping cough _____
Tetanus _____
Polio _____
Smallpox _____
Measles, mumps, rubella _____
Boosters _____
Tests _____

Illnesses _____
_____
_____
_____
_____
_____

Hospitalization _____

Beloved, I wish above all things that thou mayest prosper and be in health, even as thy soul prospereth (3 John 2).

Virtues—mom's a doll, or at least she ought to be

By the time the baby is six months old, you will probably have discovered that motherhood is forever. Up until now, life has offered alternatives to just about every situation. A difficult pet could be given away, an unsatisfactory house could be sold—even an intolerable marriage could be dissolved. But motherhood goes on and on and on. For the mothering done today lives eternally through the character of future generations. It's all a matter of values.

Although both fathers and mothers give a great deal of time to their children, it's a fact of life that mothers usually give more. This is certainly not because we're more loving or generous, but simply because we're home for the most hours each day. And so, from the very moment of birth when we first hold our arms out for the baby, we're shaping a life—whether we like it or not. It is through this squirming red bundle that our dreams, our fears, our joys, and maybe our silly little idiosyncrasies will become legacy. But for now, it will be enough for most of us if we can only teach our children a few simple values.

We want them to know that a smile is lovelier than an expensive suit of clothes, that work is an honorable pleasure, that giving should always be an expression of love, that justice is treating others fairly, and that honesty is behind all great men. No wonder the Bible speaks so favorably of the virtuous woman. Who else could get these truths across to her child?

Today your baby is a picture of perfect innocence and you may think the subject of values a bit premature. I assure you it's not. For now is the time to be examining your own life. If you're anything like me it may be that some housecleaning will have to be done before you, yourself, are a suitable example for a little one to follow.

Some of us may feel like calling in a professional maintenance team to do the cleanup job, but this is really not necessary. Through sincere desire, coupled with old-fashioned elbow grease, we can get our lives in good order in no time at all. For the Christian mother, it's worth the effort required. We can't teach values to our children unless we, ourselves, hold the same values close to our heart. I learned this lesson from a dear friend.

Kay's father was a deacon in our church, her mother an active layperson. What a surprise it was to all of us when Kay began to turn from the ways of God to join a rather rough gang of teenagers. One day I overheard an older woman passing judgment on the sad situation. "What a disappointment that child must be to her wonderful parents."

At that moment, I felt so sorry for Kay's mother and father that my heart actually ached. Many years later, however, I discovered the real story. It seemed that these people who appeared to love God so much on Sunday morning were only giving lip service to him. Once home and away from the eyes of their fellow church members, they gave in to lying, cheating, drunkenness, and just plain meanness. What they didn't realize is that they never escaped the eyes of their trusting child. Confused and misdirected, Kay did the only thing she thought she could do and still be honest. She joined a group of people who, although "rank" in character, never pretended to be anything else.

I wish I could say that all ended well in spite of the bad start Kay's parents gave her, but I can't. Kay is still out there somewhere living the life that she learned from a supposedly loving mom and dad.

Yes, the responsibility is overwhelming, and Mom's part is great. But God never intended for a mother to do it all on her own. He will work through us. We have only to turn our lives over to Christ and wait for his guidance. Christian writer Larry Christenson calls this type of living "focusing on Christ." And it is simply centering your thoughts on the Lord at all times, not just for emergencies or especially trying crises.

Each day you will pray for God's guidance, study the Scriptures for additional help, and accept his decision with love and grace. There is absolutely no need for you to spend time and money on elaborate child-care seminars. (Although there's no harm in them if you continue to leave the final authority up to Christ.) And there is no need to compare your family life with that of more liberal households. Your family is walking with the Lord and only his opinion counts.

I can't promise you a trouble-free existence just because you're working alongside of God. I can't even say for sure that you'll always be happy. But I will go so far as to say that a mother who honors the Lord enough to teach her children Christian values will have a deep sense of peace in her heart *most* of the time. Perhaps it's because she's following his will.

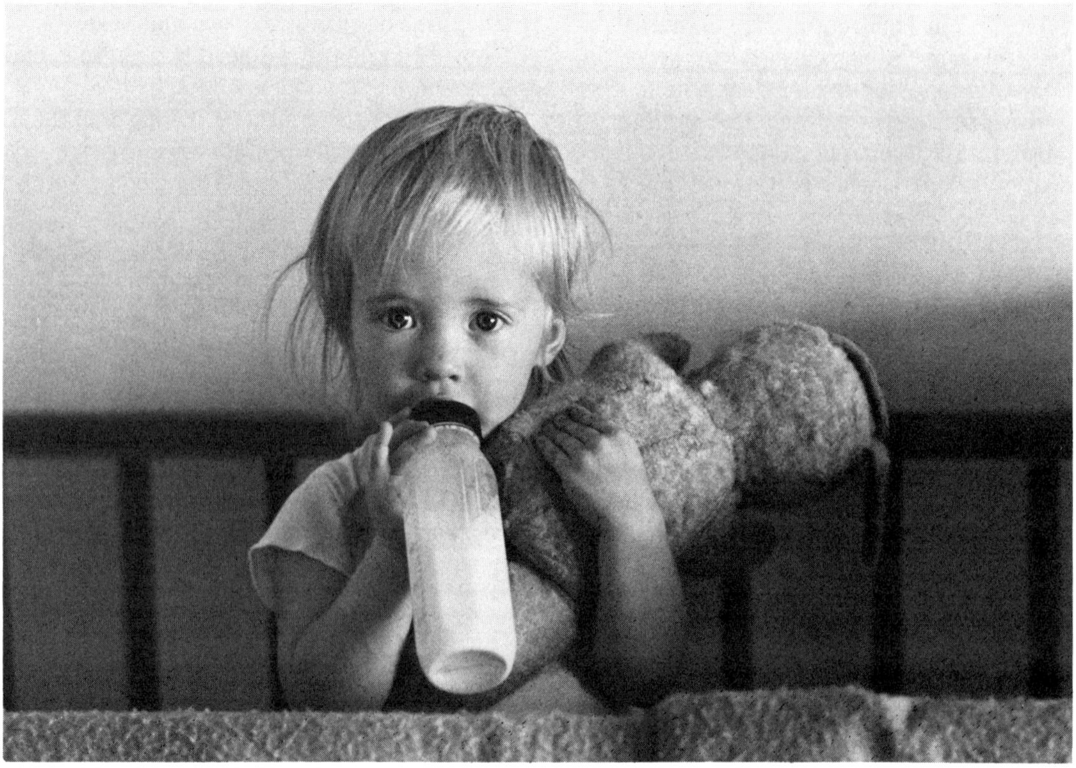

Weaning—a mother's bill of rights

"Seems like you've been nursing forever. When are you going to wean that baby?" Sarah's best friend questioned. Her own two-year-old had just walked into the room with an old plastic bottle clutched lovingly to his breast.

"Mil?" he politely asked.

Sarah waited patiently until her friend had filled the bottle, handed it to the child, and sat down again. Then she said, "So, when are *you* going to wean your baby, Martha?"

Sound typical? It's funny, but while most people don't mind seeing an older baby on the bottle, they're aghast at the mere thought of a nursing toddler. This attitude probably results from the fact that breastfeeding itself is still somewhat of a novelty in our country.

Perhaps in a few years there will have been such significant changes in our child-care philosophy that nursing an older baby will be "old hat." Until then, you can expect a lot of criticism and advice on weaning—most of it bad. Take these suggestions with as much grace as you can, then do what you want to. Weaning is a very personal matter that can only be handled between you and your baby. One day both of you will instinctively know that you're ready to step out into the world as two different people. Then, and only then, is it time for weaning.

Most mothers like to just leave it all up to baby. Such natural weaning rarely takes place before a baby is about nine months old, when he can handle a cup pretty much on his own and is eating solids well. Sometimes it happens rather quickly with baby deciding almost overnight that he's too big for nursing. And sometimes it occurs slowly and gradually, with baby dropping one feeding at a time until he's down to a nightcap and then none at all.

Many of our modern mothers insist that the length of one's nursing experience is an indication of her mothering skills. What a shame that we've allowed women to do this to breastfeeding, thereby frightening a great number of mothers away. (Besides, most babies are not interested in the breast much past their first birthday anyway.)

If your toddler does seem reluctant to give up his nursing time with you, and you haven't any objections, sit back and enjoy these "bonus" days. On the other hand, should you find that you're ready for weaning before baby, go ahead. There's nothing to be gained in resentful nursing, for a happy, well-adjusted mother and marriage is worth far more to your child than a few more months of breast milk.

If you've decided to give your baby a gentle nudge toward weaning, you can still take it slowly and naturally. Don't refuse the breast—simply don't offer it at one feeding per week. This might be the early morning nursing the first week, the afternoon snack the second week, and so forth. If baby is ready to forego nursing, he'll never even realize what you're doing—and if he does, then he's not quite ready. Let up on your efforts and try again in a week or two. It may help to keep baby occupied during his former nursing time. Try reading a book or simply playing with him for a few minutes, and remember to anticipate his hunger by offering a cup of milk and a nutritious snack before he's had time to become ravenous.

It is your right:
1. To wean your baby when you want to.
2. To wean gradually. A doctor's instructions to wean abruptly should be double-checked with another physician.

If you're being pressured about weaning, bear in mind:
1. Nursing is more than feeding—it's mothering. Sure, formula can be tolerated well by a healthy six-month-old, but that bottle doesn't offer the warmth of your arms, the smell of your body, or the touch of your skin to the same extent that breastfeeding does.
2. For as long as baby is nursing he'll be receiving valuable immunities.
3. Nursing fills you with maternal feelings that might be more than welcome when sharing a house with a toddler.
4. Nursing is the best and easiest way to soothe a child who is ill, teething, or suffering from a minor "hurt."

Weaning often leaves Mom a little sad, for she realizes her baby is growing up. But the nice thing about natural weaning is that it gives both of you the chance to adjust to separation. Usually by the time weaning is completed, baby is ready to go out and explore the world, and you're ready to rediscover yourself as a woman.

"God bless your mother—the womb from which you came, and the breasts

that gave you suck!" . . . *"Yes, but even more blessed are all who hear the Word of God and put it into practice"* (Luke 11:27, 28, TLB).

Working—working out working

To work or not to work? You'd think by now we mothers would have resolved this question. But we haven't. Those of us who are working are still feeling guilty about leaving the nest, and those of us staying at home are still remorseful about that money we're not earning. We Christian women are particularly concerned with the problem of finding our place in life. Our reasons for returning to work after having a baby are much like anybody else's —to continue with a satisfying career or to ease a financial strain, while our reasons for choosing homemaking over a career are usually child centered. It all sounds so easy, but I assure you, it's not.

Before Heather was born, I vowed that my husband and I would never change our life style. "We'll just let the baby fit into our lives instead of fitting ourselves into the baby's life," I said. But, of course, after I had held that tiny infant in my arms and witnessed her introduction to pain, hunger, and loneliness, it was suddenly a very different story. Motherhood, once only a delightful dream, was now a reality, and my role as a mother had become very clear.

But the maternal instinct doesn't always work so quickly, and simply knowing that one woman has solved the problem won't make it any easier on you—unless you were harboring her point of view in the first place. Like so many other difficult decisions, when it comes to choosing between a career and full-time mothering, you have to make up your own mind, and you have to be aware that what's right for the lady next door may not be at all suitable for you. There are, however, at least two truths that should be openly acknowledged before making a decision.

1. Children do not ask to be born.
2. Children have a right to expect both a mother and a home.

Most mothers admit that it would be best to stay at home with their baby, but where does that leave those who have to add to the family income? Not long ago, when a family needed a financial boost, the husband took up moonlighting—a part-time job in addition to his regular full-time one. Today, women don't feel that husbands owe the family an income. When money starts getting tight, chances are that the couple will jointly decide upon the wife's helping out. And this is usually good, for it leaves the husband time to be a family man. But when a mother has to earn money, both parents should strive to find a way of supplementing the income without causing her to forfeit her right to motherhood.

It might be comforting to some women to know that combining a career with homemaking is, in fact, biblical. King Lemuel describes such a situation to his son as he talks of the perfect wife.

> *She finds wool and flax and busily spins it. She buys imported foods, brought by ship from distant ports. She gets up before dawn to prepare breakfast for her household, and plans the day's work for her servant girls. She goes out to inspect a field, and buys it; with her own hands she plants a vineyard. She is energetic, a hard worker, and watches for bargains. She works far into the night. She sews for the poor, and generously gives to the needy. She has no fear of winter for her household, for she has made warm clothes for all of them. She also upholsters with finest tapestry; her own clothing is beautifully made—a purple gown of pure linen.... She makes belted linen garments to sell to the merchants. She is a woman of strength and dignity, and has no fear of old age. When she speaks, her words are wise, and kindness is the rule for everything she says. She watches carefully all that goes on throughout her household, and is never lazy. Her children stand and bless her; so does her husband* (Proverbs 31:13-22, 24-28, TLB).

No one could accuse this woman of sitting at home twiddling her thumbs. But notice that although she did indeed take part in monetary matters, she also took care of her family.
If you can manage your career and your home life in such a way that there's still time to prepare hot meals, sew your family's clothing, grow your own vegetables, and teach your children the Word of God, then more power to you. A lot of women would like your secret. In the meantime, the rest of us had better turn to a part-time job.

PART-TIME WORK

Baby-sitting. Of all the part-time positions to be considered, baby-sitting is often the most lucrative. With so many women wanting to work these days, you have only to mention your intentions to the most talkative member of the neighborhood, and bingo—you're in business. New mothers do best to start off with a preschooler who will spend mornings in front of the television and leave her with free time for baby care.

As you become more capable, you can increase your earnings by adding children one at a time until you've reached your quota. But don't be misled into thinking baby-sitting is easy. You'll be coping with children who are without the security of home and mother, and your patience will have to work overtime.

Sometimes, baby-sitting just doesn't work out. Perhaps the children never adjust to your family, or you frankly can't manage another child in addition to your own. There are other alternatives to working away from home. Choose from the following:

Sewing. A good seamstress is always in demand. If you don't believe it, try putting a card up on the bulletin board at a local fabric shop and wait for the deluge of calls that are sure to come.

Baking. Take orders from neighbors for specialty breads. A good wholesome bread made from soy flour is usually a hard one for anybody to resist. Once you're on your feet, a health card is easily obtained and allows you to sell on a more public level.

Manuscript typing. If you live near a college or university and can type, consider yourself in a gold mine. An advertisement in the school newspaper is all you need to get started, but take note that perfection is a must in this area.

Door-to-door sales. Cosmetics, jewelry, and even clothing items are being sold in this manner now, and the nice thing about it is that you can take your baby right along with you during the day and still share the evenings with your husband.

Children's parties. Grab a partner and begin hostessing children's birthday parties. A simple endeavor like this could develop into catering for adult gatherings or even weddings.

Telephone sales. Only the very brave should tackle telephone work, but if you can tolerate anger from the other end of the receiver and not take it out on your family, it's worth a try.

Once-a-year fund raiser. In need of extra cash for Christmas or a special birthday? Garage sales, plant sales, and craft sales are sure bets. One woman I know throws an annual Calico Christmas Sale. By spending the summer making Christmas ornaments from scraps of calico, she is able to lay aside a sizable nest egg for her own Christmas.

Outside work. Don't completely overlook working outside of the home. When part-time work pays well enough to compensate for the baby-sitter, it can be a very satisfactory experience.

Of course, there are some women who feel they need the fulfillment of a career. Would it surprise you to learn that this includes most of us? Maybe a fresh look at motherhood itself would help things, for a mother does have a career. She is self-employed in the field of household management, and her duties don't stop with child care and house maintenance. She's dietician, seamstress, counselor, nurse, teacher, gardener, entertainer, and a great deal more. Like all jobs, motherhood does require a period of training and adjustment, and it's during this time that so many women decide nothing could be worse than "keeping house."

If you hope to find happiness in homemaking, you'll first of all have to relax your attitude about life. Time will seem to move slower now, and yet it'll take forever to get anything accomplished.

All at once, your goals must become simpler —a successful day may mean that you've done little more than put a roast on the table. But what a joy being your own boss is. It gives you the right to play with baby as much as you like, to visit with friends, to arrange your own schedule, or to even take a holiday.

Afraid of stagnating? Learn something new each month. Canning, needlework, and furniture refinishing are just a sampling of projects that few working women have time to pursue. When the walls seem to be coming in on you, consider signing up for a Mother's Day Out program at your church. This service allows mothers to have one whole day off each week while their children are under Christian supervision. You might also look into evening classes at the closest university. However, be careful not to get in over your head—a baby doesn't leave much study time.

Another nice way to learn and socialize at the same time is to enroll in adult education classes. You can take up weaving, knitting, powderpuff mechanics, and much more without the pressure of grades.

There will definitely be days on which you ask yourself, "Why am I bothering to play the housewife scene?"

And you need to be able to answer this before those bad days hit. Are you staying home just so your child can take naps in his own bed? Play with his own toys? Eat your home-cooked meals? Be protected from the cold germs that cause such havoc in day-care centers? No, although certainly any one of these reasons would be enough in itself to justify your presence at home. It's because you, a Christian mother, want to raise your child in an atmosphere of Christian love.

Sure, motherhood is at times a sacrifice, but it's also the greatest joy of living. That's why in spite of the wonderful advances that the women's movement has brought us, I hope my daughter will one day say, "When I grow up, I want to be a mommy."

XYZ's of family fun

To every thing there is a season, and a time to every purpose under the heaven: A time to weep, and a time to laugh; a time to mourn, and a time to dance (Ecclesiastes 3:1, 4).

Celebrations are important. Not only are they just plain fun, they work miraculously in reviving low spirits. Now that you're a family, celebrating will from necessity take on a different shape from those old twosome days. Instead of splurging on a fancy dinner out, you'll discover that setting the table with your best china adds the same festive touch. Instead of celebrating your engagement date, you'll turn all of baby's "firsts" into grand occasions. And instead of waiting for a real cause to party, celebrating itself becomes reason enough.

Mothers have an inborn knack for realizing

when everyday living must replace fun and games. The hardest part is in knowing how to make these days special and apart from all others. Many mothers claim that the secret lies in having an inexhaustible supply of holidays to celebrate. When the calendar is uncooperative, these women simply invent their own. Anything and everything is a holiday. And although few of us will get into the spirit well enough to celebrate a lost job, we can easily see the fun behind a first snow party or a new tooth festival.

A YEAR OF FUN

Below is a whole year of holidays and interesting ways to spend your time. Go ahead and try them all out—a family is at its best when having fun.

January. A good month to rest, read, and indulge in craft sets you might have received as Christmas gifts. Feeling blue? Treat yourself to a single carnation.
Special day—
    January 1 (New Year's Day)

February. A month of celebrations. Why not decorate the house with pretty valentines, invest in heart-shaped cookie cutters, and make these twenty-eight days a real change of pace.
Special days—
    February 2 (Ground Hog Day)
    February 12 (Lincoln's Birthday)
    February 14 (Valentine's Day)
    February 22 (Washington's Birthday)

March. A nice month for flying kites, having a dinner party, and adding a touch of spring to your house via a bright tablecloth or colorful house plant.
Special days—
    March 13 (Chinese holiday—Queen of All Flowers' Birthday)
    March 15 (Ides of March)
    March 17 (St. Patrick's Day)
    March 30 (1858—First pencil with an eraser patented. Celebrate by giving your friends a jumbo pencil.)

April. New beginnings are in the air. In addition to celebrating Easter, use this month for getting summer wardrobes in order.
Special days—
    April 1 (April Fools Day)
    April 4 (Commemoration of Dr. Martin Luther King)
    April 15 (Income tax due)
    According to the moon—Palm Sunday, Good Friday, and Easter

May. A pleasant month for outdoor activities. Picnics, bike rides, and backpacking are lovely ways to welcome in the warm weather.
Special days—
    May 1 (May Day)
    Second Sunday (Mother's Day)
    Third Saturday (Armed Forces Day)
    May 30 (Memorial Day)

June. Cook-out time. Save on energy—both yours and the electric company's—by grilling dinner as often as possible. Outdoor barbeques are a good way to get to know those neighbors as well.
Special days—
    June 12 (Children's Day)
    June 14 (Flag Day)
    Third Sunday (Father's Day)
    June 21 (Summer begins)

July. A great month for investing in a child's swimming pool. Spend the hottest part of the day in air-conditioned comfort, and make sure that both you and baby drink plenty of cool liquids. Homemade ice cream, anyone?
Special days—
    July 4 (Independence Day)
    July 20 (1969—First landing on the moon)
    July 23 (1904—Ice cream cone was introduced)

August. Summer ends. Take advantage of these sun-filled days by camping and boating. Begin thinking about fall clothing and the

wonders you can do with a sewing machine.
Special days—
>August 18 (1587—Virginia Dare, first English child born in America. Why not have a birthday party?)

September. A settling down to business month. Make new plans for yourself. Join a Bible study group, sign up for art lessons, or dedicate yourself to some worthy cause.
Special days—
>First Monday (Labor Day)
>September 23 (Autumn begins)
>According to locality—school starts

October. Winter days are soon to come. This is the time to enjoy brisk evening walks and begin your leaf collecting for autumn centerpieces. As All Saints Eve approaches, remember, adults enjoy costume parties too!
Special days—
>October 12 (Columbus Day)
>October 31 (All Saints Eve)

November. Thoughts of holidays are everywhere. Prepare your own household for the Christmas season by making plans as to what you'll bake, what you'll give, and where you'll go. These first cold days make a restful time to catch up on correspondence.
Special days—
>First Tuesday (General Election Day)
>November 11 (Veteran's Day)
>November 19 (1863—Lincoln's Gettysburg Address)
>Fourth Thursday (Thanksgiving Day)

December. A month of fun and festivity. Do remember to take time for prayer and Scripture reading. Christ is what this holiday is all about.
Special days—
>December 22 (Winter begins)
>December 24 (Christmas Eve)
>December 25 (Christmas Day)
>December 31 (New Year's Eve)

PHOTO CREDITS
Jim Steere *front cover*
William Koechling *pages 14, 20, 28, 34, 56, 64, 80, 88, 111, 128, 141*
Jim Whitmer *page 16*
Bob Combs *pages 40, 50, 68-69, 118, 132*
Timothy Botts *pages 42, 63, 82*
Rick Smolan *page 47*
Brent Jones *pages 58, 96, 137*
Robert McKendrick *pages 70, 104*
Jayne Garrison *page 116*